SHOOTER'S GUIDE to
SHOTGUNS

TERRY WIELAND

Published by

Gun Digest® Books, an imprint of F+W Media, Inc.
Krause Publications • 700 East State Street • Iola, WI 54990-0001
715-445-2214 • 888-457-2873
www.krausebooks.com

To order books or other products call toll-free 1-800-258-0929
or visit us online at www.gundigeststore.com

ISBN-13: 978-1-4402-3463-7
ISBN-10: 1-4402-3463-9

Edited by Jennifer L.S. Pearsall
Cover Design by Al West
Designed by Nicole MacMartin

Printed in USA

For

James Guthrie
1975 – 2013

No Better Friend

CONTENTS

ABOUT THE AUTHOR

Terry Wieland is a highly respected shotgun expert. He has been handling and hunting with shotguns for nearly 50 years and has taken game and broken clays with these tools on several continents. He is the author of hundreds of magazine articles and nine books on shooting, two of which are specifically devoted to shotguns and shotgunning. He is a regular contributor to *Gray's Sporting Journal, Shooting Sportsman, Petersen's Shotguns, The Contemporary Sportsman,* and *The Contemporary Wingshooter.* He has been the Shooting Editor of *Gray's Sporting Journal* since 1993, and has been a regular contributor to our own annual *Gun Digest* volume for many, many years.

INTRODUCTION

The shotgun is the oldest of firearms, the most widely used in the world today, and the most useful and versatile overall. A shotgun is also the most fun to shoot.

Historically, shotguns have also been referred to as "smoothbores," to differentiate them from rifled firearms, and also "scatterguns," to denote shot that scatters in a pattern, rather than a firearm that fires a single projectile. By whatever name, shotguns have myriad uses: Hunting both large and small game, self-defense and tactical applications (including use by police and military), and a wide variety of games and sports from informal hand traps in the backyard to Olympic competition.

Obviously, a gun intended for any of these purposes is not necessarily suited to others. A typical gun for rabbit hunting on a farm, for example, is not ideal for shooting Olympic trap. Having said that, we must also add that a single shotgun can be made to do more things well than can any other type of firearm; there is such a thing as an "all-around" shotgun that allows its owner to participate in many different activities and to turn in good performances in all of them.

With so many varieties and with shotguns made for a host of activities in many different countries, the newcomer looking to buy a gun can be forgiven for feeling completely lost. Even shotgun veterans can be confused by the myriad guns and configurations now available, to say nothing of the variety of shotshells for them.

This guide is intended to help sort them all out: to assist a father in buying a first shotgun for a son or daughter, whether for hunting or to participate in collegiate shooting sports; for a new shotgunner to purchase the right gun to start with; or for a shooter with some years under their belt and a desire to move into other disciplines and procuring the right second or third gun. We hope even shotgunners of many years' experience will find this book interesting and informative. With shotguns, there is always something new to learn, a different activity to master, a different skill to polish. That's what has made shotgunning popular for 200 years, and it's what keeps us all coming back.

Missouri shooters Ryan Mason and Alison Caselman compete in skeet, trap, and sporting clays. They appear throughout this book demonstrating guns and techniques.

CHAPTER 1

THE SHOTGUN IN HISTORY

What is a shotgun? Very simply, a shotgun is a firearm that shoots many small projectiles at one time. Unlike a rifle, which seeks to place a single bullet in an exact spot on the target, a shotgun fires a charge of round-shaped pellets that expand in a cloud as the charge leaves the muzzle. While the rifle is a long-range weapon, accurate out to several hundred yards and beyond, the shotgun is used at short range and is normally effective from 20 to 60 yards at the most. Unlike other firearms, the shotgun is intended for use primarily on moving targets, such as a flying bird or a running rabbit.

An early break-action hammer side-by-side shotgun, by Holland & Holland.

Although its exact origins are lost far back in time—firearms have been with us for about 800 years—the shotgun was certainly one of the very earliest firearm forms. The shooter would pour some gunpowder down the barrel and then drop in anything that came to hand, from pebbles to scrap iron. All early firearms were very short-range propositions, and such shrapnel could be extremely effective.

Early guns were very crude. Although some were intended for firing while held in the hands, they were constructed with neither accuracy nor convenience in mind. The barrel was a piece of pipe, the stock merely a chunk of iron or wood that served as a handle. The refined technical features of a gun we now take for granted, including the stock, the lock mechanism for firing, and the trigger to trip the lock, evolved over hundreds of years.

The story of firearms development has filled hundreds of books, and we don't have space here for any but a quick look. However, to understand the shotgun as it now exists, as well as the demands it places on the shooter, it is useful to know how it works and why.

The force used to propel bullets or pellets out of a firearm is provided by expanding gases. These gases come from burning gunpowder, either the original blackpowder or today's smokeless propellants. There are similarities and differences between the two, but the basic principle is the same: A flame

The development of driven shooting in England also drove shotgun development. Here, the "guns" wait for pheasants, at a shoot in Idaho.

Some early implements used to load blackpowder shotshells. Today's cartridges are, of course, much easier to use.

is applied to the gunpowder and, as the gunpowder burns, it creates gas that expands rapidly, applying pressure to the projectile and hurling it out of the muzzle at high speed.

Gunpowder is not an explosive in the technical meaning of the term. Smokeless powder, such as we use in modern shotshells, is correctly called a "propellant." Different powders are used for different purposes, mostly based on burning rate. The pressure peak in a modern shotshell is in the neighborhood of 10,000 pounds per square inch (psi). Obviously, such pressures can be very destructive, if not confined by good steel. For this reason, shooters must be aware of the loads they use in their guns, and handloaders (those who load their own shotshells), must ensure they use the correct powder in the proper amount.

To anyone familiar with pressures and how they make things function in everything from cars to hydraulics, it is obvious you cannot simply pour some blackpowder down a gun barrel, throw the lead pellets in

afterwards, and expect to fire a shot. The expanding gas would blow right through the pile of pellets. A device was required to create a seal between the gunpowder and the shot charge, to confine and direct the pressure. In muzzleloaders, this was done with a cloth or paper patch called a "wad."

The other major problem back a couple centuries was in how to ignite the powder. The early methods of the match- and wheellock, which used a smoldering fuse to touch the powder, were eventually replaced by the flintlock. In that mechanism, a piece of flint is held in a hammer. When released by the trigger, the hammer swings forward and the flint strikes steel, creating a rain of sparks, and these ignite a small charge of gunpowder in a part called the "pan." Flames then flash through an opening in the barrel, the "flash hole," igniting the main charge of gunpowder.

This was the state of the shotgun in 1800. A shooter would pour a couple drams of powder down the muzzle, seat a wad over

A hammer gun by J. Woodward & Sons of London, made for blackpowder and still an exceedingly fine game gun.

it, pour in some shot, and seat another wad over that to hold it in place. He would then pour a pinch of powder into the flintlock's pan and close the frizzen (lid). When he wanted to fire, he brought the gun to his shoulder, thumbing back the hammer as he did so, then pointed the gun and pulled the trigger. The hammer swung forward and, after what seems to us today to be an interminable delay, the gun would fire.

By modern standards, this was a slow process from start to finish. Speed, not only of loading but of firing, from the time the trigger was tripped until the pellets exited the muzzle, was the critical factor that severely restricted the uses of the shotgun at that time. Compared to the wheellock, however, the flintlock was quite fast—fast

enough to allow the shooter to bring down flying birds. This new sport was called "shooting-flying."

Shooting-flying originated in France, in the 1700s, and, by 1800, was well developed. The practice migrated to England, where gunners began to shoot birds in the air via a number of manners. One was the original trap shooting, wherein the shooter killed a live pigeon released from a trap of some kind.

The earliest live-pigeon matches were recorded in England, in 1793. Almost from the beginning, pigeon shooting competitions involved prize money and heavy betting. With large sums at stake, shooters began to pay more attention to the guns they used, how they worked, how reliable

Joseph Manton and his older brother, John, are credited with being the gun makers who did the most to turn the muzzleloader from a crude implement into a fine tool.

The flintlocks of a Joseph Manton fowling piece.

they were, and how easy they were to use. Ease of use depended on the fit of the gun; for the first time, the idea arose of matching a gun's shape and dimensions to the physique of the shooter.

Gun making was already well advanced in London. In the era of the Brown Bess musket, when all shoulder arms were relatively crude, the one firearm to which all gentlemen paid close attention was the dueling pistol. As a result, the first makers of "fine" guns specialized in dueling pistols and refined them in terms of both mechanism and workmanship. With the advent of pigeon shooting, they began to apply the same care to the "fowling piece."

The Manton brothers, Joseph and John, are credited with being the first gun makers to regard the fowling piece as a fine instrument, rather than a crude tool. The Mantons refined the shape of gun stocks and paid close attention to their guns' overall balance. Every piece of the gun was carefully filed, polished, and fitted, and their guns were recognized as works of functional art.

Not only did the Mantons change society's view of guns themselves, in their efforts, they trained many fine craftsmen who later went into business and grew into the society of London gun makers who have gone down in history. These included, among others, James Purdey, Charles Lancaster, and Thomas Boss.

Until 1800, there was little difference between a rifle and a shotgun. A musket could be loaded to shoot either a single projectile or many, whether the barrel was rifled or not. "Rifling" is a series of grooves that impart spin to a projectile and make it more accurate, like fletching on an arrow. A shotgun, on the other hand, generally has a smooth bore (although there are some exceptions). After the Mantons, the evolution of the fowling piece began in earnest, enough that it came to be recognized as a completely different animal than the rifle.

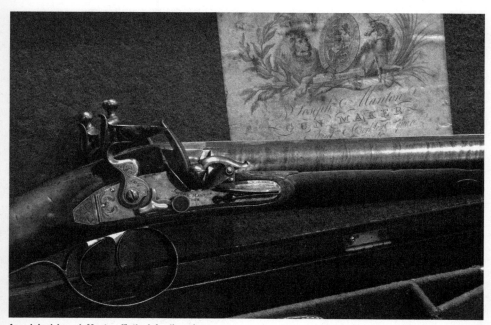

An original Joseph Manton flintlock fowling piece.

The American Spencer shotgun was the earliest slide-action design. Compared to double guns, it was heavy and clumsy, but pump guns were quickly refined into more usable forms.

The next major breakthrough came, in 1807, with the invention of percussion ignition by the Reverend Alexander Forsyth, a Scottish clergyman with an interest in chemistry. Instead of flint, sparks, and fine gunpowder, percussion priming ignited a chemical compound with a sharp blow. The priming compound was contained in a small cap. This was placed over a nipple, which enclosed the flash hole, and was ignited by a blow from the gun's hammer.

Percussion guns were both faster and more convenient than flintlocks, and the development of wingshooting proceeded in parallel with the evolution of the guns themselves. As firearms became quicker to operate and more ergonomic in design, shooters found new ways of using them. By 1840, wingshooting was well established in England.

The marriage of Queen Victoria to her German cousin, Prince Albert, was a turn-

Lever-action shotguns were developed because of the popularity of lever rifles, but they never gained a large share of the market.

Some of the many different shotshells offered by Holland & Holland over the years, on display at the company's shooting grounds outside London.

ing point both for shooting in England and for the development of the shotgun. Prince Albert was an enthusiastic hunter and shooter, and people of all classes followed his lead. With demand high and money plentiful, English gun makers embarked on a frenzy of development that began with the Great Exhibition of 1851 (also credited to Prince Albert, whose idea it was), and the subsequent development and refinement of break-action shotguns and centerfire cartridges. Although both the pinfire cartridge and the breechloading gun appeared in France well before 1851, it was the English—especially the English upper classes—who drove shotgun development from that point forward.

By 1870, the shotgun had progressed from percussion muzzleloaders to break-action pinfires, and from there to central-fire mechanisms and self-contained cartridges. Driven shooting, the shooting of birds that are pushed by beaters and flushed over a line of waiting guns, had become a national mania. The great names of English gun making—Purdey, Woodward, Lancaster, Boss, Westley Richards—were inventing and producing at a rate never seen before or since. Among them, they refined the double-barreled shotgun into what we have today and set a standard for quality that even now can hardly be matched.

* * *

In America, wingshooting developed differently, the American shotgun along different lines. "Market gunners," professionals shooting ducks, geese, and other birds for the commercial food and feather markets, demanded firepower. Although

The pinfire was the first practical breechloader and a perfectly usable game gun. Many remained in use long after the centerfire cartridge took over. This modern pinfire cartridge is made from a conventional brass centerfire hull.

America did make some conventional double shotguns, like the Lefever and Parker, its major contribution came in the form of repeating shotguns, such as the pump and, later, the semi-automatic.

Through the 1870s and '80s, America was a major export market for English gun makers; having an English gun was a gentleman's status symbol. Firms like W&C Scott and W.W. Greener supplied the recreational shooting market in America, while American gun makers supplied guns for the market gunners. By 1900, shotguns were being used for so many different activities and made in so many different forms, it becomes difficult to describe their evolution in broad terms. This variety was made possible because of the simultaneous development of centerfire cartridges.

The centerfire cartridge that replaced the pinfire, around 1870, consisted of all the same elements as a percussion muzzleloader: gunpowder, wads, shot, and a primer to ignite the powder. The difference was, it was all contained in the wondrous little mechanism we now refer to as a "shotshell."

In 1870, shotshells were filled with blackpowder, the original mixture of saltpeter, sulfur, and charcoal. Gradually, through the 1880s and '90s, blackpowder was displaced by various types of "smokeless" powders, chemical mixtures usually based on nitroglycerine. They had different burning patterns, burned more cleanly, and generated higher pressures and velocities than their blackpowder predecessors.

With the centerfire shotshell perfected, shotgun inventors were free to design all manner of mechanisms to shoot them. These included not only the conventional break-action double guns, but also guns with magazines to hold the shotshells and

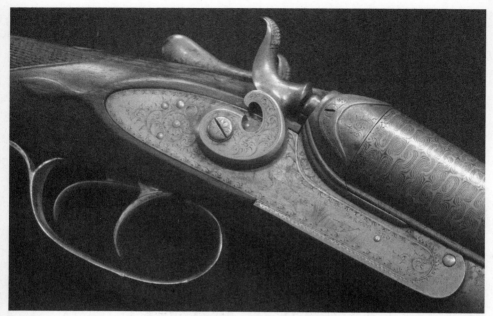

An early Parker hammer gun with Damascus barrels. The Parker was one of the first, and is now the most iconic, of American shotguns.

guns with different methods of chambering them and ejecting empty cases, including lever-actions, slide-actions (pumps) and bolt-actions. Although there were no technical objections to any of these, there were limitations imposed by the gun's use.

The British, catering to shooters involved in such intensely competitive realms as live pigeons and driven pheasants, realized early that there was more to a good shotgun than firepower. How a gun could be handled and swung was extremely important, if the shooter wanted to hit anything consistently. Because a shotgun does not have sights and is pointed, rather than aimed, a gun has to fit the shooter at least reasonably well and the barrel line up naturally with his eye, if he is to have consistent success.

By 1900, the different sizes of shotguns had also been established. Evolving as they did from muzzleloaders, shotguns continued to use much of the same terminology. Today, we think of shotguns as 12-gauge,

or 20-gauge, or 16s or .410s. All except the .410 grew from the antiquated fashion of describing a shotgun bore by its diameter. A 12-gauge, for example, is .729-inch, because that is the diameter of a lead sphere weighing exactly one-twelfth of a pound. The 16-gauge is the diameter of a lead sphere that is one-sixteenth (one ounce exactly), the 20 is one-twentieth, and so on. This is why the larger the number, the smaller the bore. The exception is the .410, which is a caliber, not a gauge. It has a bore that is .410-inch in diameter.

Historically, shotguns ranged from 2-bores (projectiles weighing a half-pound) down to odd sizes measured in millimeters (a 9mm shotgun has a bore about .357-inch). For waterfowling, the British also used large, boat-mounted guns called "punt guns." These were permanently installed on small fowling boats in the manner of the mounted guns of a battleship. American market gunners also used

The showroom at Connecticut Shotgun Manufacturing Co., in New Britain, Connecticut. Owner Antony Galazan not only manufactures fine guns, he also deals in all manner of shotguns from centuries past. An hour in his showroom is like visiting history.

punt guns, which were eventually outlawed along with the practice of market gunning; the last reported seizure of a punt gun took place in the 1930s, on Chesapeake Bay. Such sporting artillery is really outside the scope of this book, but it shows that shotguns come in all shapes and sizes.

For the wingshooter who wants a gun he can carry comfortably, mount to the shoulder easily, and swing smoothly, while not being battered by excessive recoil no matter how many shots he may fire, the practical gauges were narrowed to six: 10, 12, 16, 20, 28, and .410. In America, market gunners had used 8-gauge guns, but those were outlawed for hunting use along with the commercial trade in game. There were also various in-between gauges, such as the 14, 18, 24, and 32, but those fell by the wayside, simply because of conve-

nience—they offered nothing that could not be obtained with the more common 12, 16, 20, and 28.

For reasons best known to themselves, the venerable English firm of Boss & Co. liked the 14-gauge and continued to produce them long after others had abandoned that size. Boss always was somewhat quirky.

In England, the 12-gauge (or 12-bore, as they call it), became the overwhelming favorite for all shotgun sports. The 12-gauge is also the worldwide trap-shooting gauge. In America, where skeet originated officially, in 1926, four gauges were designated for registered tournaments—12, 20, 28, and .410. This is the major reason for the decline in popularity and availability of 16-gauge guns and ammunition.

There are practical reasons for all this, one of which has to do with recoil. Phys-

The six dominant shotshell sizes, from left: 10-, 12-, 16-, 20-, 28-gauge, and .410-bore.

ics tells us that, for every action, there is an equal and opposite reaction. In the case of a shotgun, when the charge exits the muzzle at high speed, the gun slams back into the shoulder of the shooter. If this blow is excessive, shooting becomes painful and unpleasant and usually leads to the shooter developing a flinch. Even if one shot doesn't have this effect, a succession of lighter shots can, for the effect of recoil is cumulative. For a shotgunner to down birds or break clays consistently, he must not be afraid of his gun.

The British developed the "rule of 96," which states that the ideal weight for a gun is 96 times the weight of its shot charge. So, for a gun like a 16-gauge firing one ounce of shot, the gun should weigh 96 ounces, or exactly six pounds. A 12-gauge firing 1$\frac{1}{8}$ ounces should weigh 6$\frac{3}{4}$ pounds.

Shotguns, more than any other firearm, are subject to the immutable laws of physics, with each element—shot charge, shot size, velocity, gun weight, barrel length, and so on—having an effect on other elements. These aspects will be explored in detail in later chapters, but, for now, suffice it to say that the basic aspect of shotgunning that governs everything else is the flight characteristics of a round, lead pellet. These laws and characteristics have not changed since the modern shotgun emerged 150 years ago, and no technological breakthrough ever will change them. Shotgunners and shotgun makers are dealing with the same challenges today as were the great gun makers of the mid-1800s. That is what makes the shotgun such a fascinating (and sometimes infuriating) implement.

CHAPTER 2

SHOOTING THE SHOTGUN

Dynamic motion: Three quail in the air, and the gun and the shooter in motion. Only the pointer is frozen.

I n order to know what kind of shotgun will work best for you, it is important to understand how a shotgun is normally used. The most important single fact is that a shotgun is used primarily for shooting moving targets. It is a dynamic weapon and, in use, the target, the gun, and the shooter are all in motion.

A shotgun does not have fixed sights. Although there may be various arrangements of beads and ribs along the barrel that are intended as sighting aids, the shooter does not consciously align them with the target before pulling the trigger. Instead, the eyes watch the target while the hands guide the shotgun to it, just as you might point your finger at a flying bird.

As with most things to do with shotguns these days, there are exceptions. Tactical guns often have rifle-like sights, as do shotguns intended for big-game hunting and that use slugs. Historically, however, and this is still the case today, most shotguns are used for moving targets, whether they are game birds, running rabbits, or clay pigeons.

The stock of this Galazan A-10 Sporting Gun is adjustable for drop at comb, as well as length of pull.
Photo by John Giammatteo

The use of shotguns with slugs or buckshot, either for self-defense or specialized hunting as for deer, is more akin to rifle shooting than it is to conventional shotgun use. Since most people starting out with a shotgun want to shoot some sort of flying target, it is important to understand this, in order to know what to look for in a shotgun.

The English, who have taken both wingshooting and the making of shotguns to the level of fine art, place great emphasis on "fit." They believe a shotgun should fit the shooter in a manner that ensures the eyes, hands, and gun barrel are aligned properly in order to hit a flying target consistently. Obviously, a gun that is the right size for a stout, six-foot man with long arms will not fit a thin, five-foot woman with shorter arms and small hands.

In America, most shotguns are mass produced in standard sizes, and shooters have adapted themselves to whatever gun they happen to have. At various times, however, some manufacturers have produced what are called "women" and "youth" models. These guns will be lighter, with shorter stocks and barrels.

The most important dimension in shotgun fit is the length of the stock. Measured straight back from the center of the trigger to the center of the butt, this is called "length of pull" (LOP). Typically, a gun will have a LOP of 14 to 14½ inches.

The next important dimension is "drop." If you lay a straight edge along the barrel and extending out over the buttstock, and measure the distance down from the straight edge to the upper edge of the stock at the butt, you determine the drop. How much or little drop a stock has determines whether the eyes are high or low and, as a result, whether the gun shoots high or low in relation to where the shooter is looking. There are further refinements of measurement, including bend to left or right (cast-on or cast-off), according to whether the shooter is left- or right-handed, but pull and drop are the two most important. Anyone buying a new gun can expect to get more or less standard dimensions to which the average person can adapt, but the buyer of a used gun should be careful to ensure the stock has not been altered (cut off, lengthened, or bent to any degree), thereby making it unsuitable for him.

At the upper levels of pricing, guns costing $10,000 and more are usually made to the custom dimensions of the buyer. These dimensions are determined by having measurements taken by a qualified shotgun fitter. Like a tailor measuring you for a suit of clothes, a shotgun fitter uses a gun with an adjustable stock (called a "try gun"), and watches as you shoot, making adjustments here and there to move the pattern to where it is desired. When you are shooting well with it, he measures the stock, writes down the dimensions, and there you have the ideal dimensions for a gunstock fit to you.

You cannot be measured for a gun in any meaningful way by someone in a gun shop with a tape measure, nor by filling in the blanks on a chart of body measurements, nor by employing such folk lore methods as seeing if a gun held in one hand will fit into the crook of your arm. A proper shotgun measurement takes a couple hours on a range, requires a hundred shots, and costs anywhere from $250 to $400. If you are spending thousands on a gun, this is a good investment; in fact, it hardly makes sense not to do it.

Even if you have no plans to order a custom-fitted gun, knowing your ideal shotgun dimensions will help in buying a used gun or adapting an existing gun to your requirements. This can be done by bending the stock, adding a recoil pad, or moving the trigger. If you have a competition gun with an adjustable stock, you can easily alter it to your own measurements.

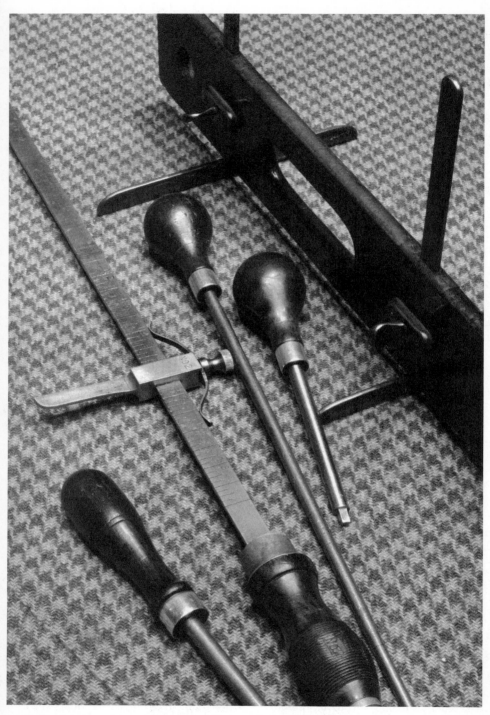

A collection of stock-measuring tools at the Holland & Holland shooting grounds outside London. Some are a century old.

In the early days, London's fine gunmakers often made their own tools and instruments, to the same quality as their guns. This is a gauge for measuring length of pull.

The interesting thing about shotgun fit is that you need to learn to shoot reasonably well before you can really be fitted for a gun. This means most of us will start out with a gun of standard dimensions—and the vast majority will shoot nothing else throughout their lives. Many will do so quite happily, downing birds and dusting clays. The truth about shotgun fit is that it is not quite so important as its proponents would have us believe, but it is far more important than we are told by those who say it simply doesn't matter.

For the beginner, a gun that is close to a proper fit is good enough to learn with. A gun that obviously does *not* fit, however, is a problem. Such a gun will be difficult to shoot, tough to learn with, and may impart a flinch or bad habits that will later be almost impossible to shake. For this reason, anyone setting out to learn to shoot a shotgun should seek the assistance of a good instructor, who will make sure he or she starts out with a suitable gun that fits, at least well enough, and learns to use it properly.

This is the aspect of shotgun shooting that is impossible to over-emphasize. Like driving a car, it is best to learn from a qualified expert. No matter how good a shot your father or brother may be, that does not mean he knows how to teach his skills to someone else. For girls and women especially, learning from a stranger is almost always easier and more productive than learning from a husband or relative.

Shooting a shotgun is an art more than a science, although science certainly enters into it. Unlike rifle shooting, where factors like bullet drop and target distance can easily be measured and allowances for bullet flight and distance defined in pure numbers, shooting a shotgun is a matter of feel—and no small degree of instinct.

Take three top-notch shotgunners and ask them how they do it, what they see

Shooting a shotgun is a dynamic process of movement: The target, the shooter, the gun, and the shot charge are all moving.

In England, shooting instruction begins at an early age. The gun is scaled down to properly fit these very young shooters, a very important consideration in learning to shoot.

Good form with a shotgun, demonstrated by competitive shooter Alison Caselman. Both eyes are open, gun is properly mounted, her leading hand is well forward, and she's leaning into the shot but is well balanced. The stock of her Blaser F3 is adjustable to give a perfect fit.

Checking shotgun fit: The height of the comb determines the height of the shooter's cheek and eye in relation to the gun and impacts where the shotgun shoots versus what the handler is seeing (either too high or too low).

when they pull the trigger, and you may get three widely differing views. On a crossing bird at 30 yards, one may say he leads the bird by six feet, another will say three, and the third may insist he shoots straight at it with no lead at all. Yet all three drop the bird. How can this be? The answer is that what we think we see and how we think we react may be quite different than what we actually see and do with a shotgun in our hands.

Simple arithmetic dictates that, if a charge of shot leaves the muzzle at 1,200 feet per second (fps), it will take a thirteenth of a second to travel 30 yards. If a pheasant is crossing in front at 30 yards, flying at 30 miles an hour (about 44 fps), then the pheasant will have travelled about 3½ feet between the pulling of the trigger and the time the shot reaches him.

Since a shot pattern comprised of an ounce of shot and fired from a Full-choke

barrel is only about 30 inches in diameter at 33 yards, the shooter has some leeway, but not much. The shooter needs to lead the bird by at least 3½ feet if he hopes to center the bird in his pattern. Yet some shooters say they lead by twice that amount, while others say they give no lead at all.

The explanation for this anomaly lies in the mysterious epicenter of shotgun shooting known as "swing." Like a batter in baseball swinging a bat to hit a moving ball, the shotgunner is swinging the gun in order to release the shot to intercept a moving target. If the swing stops or slows or speeds up too much, the result is a miss.

Swing, with a shotgun, depends on many factors, of which fit is just one. Another is weight and a third is balance. Experienced shotgunners take all of these into consideration, when choosing a new gun. Like fit itself, though, the exact

Skeet shooting: At station seven, Alison is positioned to take the bird, which has just left the low house. The other shooters are watching where they expect the bird to be broken.

Still at station seven, Alison has swung around to intercept the incoming bird from released from the high house and crossing the field to her right. Her relaxed stance allows her to pivot at the hips and swing comfortably.

The blur at the top of the wood clay house is a clay pigeon leaving the high house at skeet station No. 1 and moving nearly straight away from the shooter. The shooter has a good, relaxed stance, his weight on his leading foot.

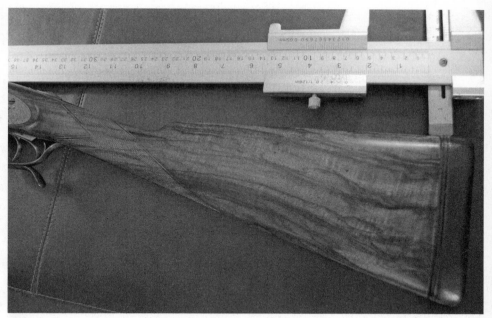

Measuring the drop of a stock at heel. This combination gauge also measures length of pull, as well as drop.

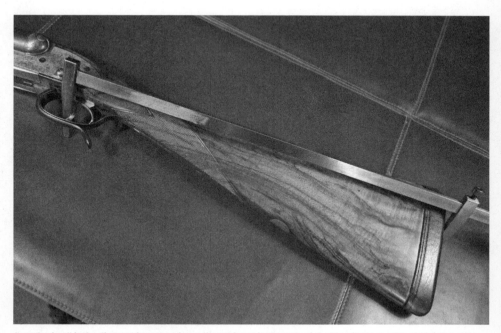

Length of pull is the distance from the trigger (front trigger, in the case of double-trigger guns) to the center of the butt. This is the single most important dimension in shotgun fit.

weight and balance that are right for you cannot really be determined until you have some experience as a shooter.

A good instructor will ensure that you start out with a gun that is appropriate to your size, shape, and strength, whose recoil will not hurt you, and with which you can reasonably expect to hit something, if your eyes are in the right place, your hands follow your eyes, and your body and arms swing through. That's all it takes.

Sounds easy, doesn't it?

CHAPTER 3

TYPES OF SHOTGUNS

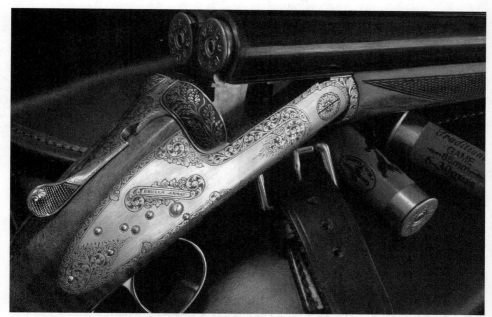

This is a Grulla Armas Windsor Woodcock, a light, 12-gauge game gun custom-made in the Basque Country of Spain.

Over the past 500 years, shotguns have been made in every conceivable configuration. In addition to the early muzzleloading guns, there are single-shots, double-barrels (with barrels aligned either vertically or horizontally), multi-barreled and combination guns, and guns that are operated by levers, bolts, or slides, as well as semi-automatic actions that operate themselves, powered either by redirected gases or their own recoil.

In America today, we commonly use five types: singles, doubles (side-by-sides and over/unders), pumps, and semi-autos. Not surprisingly, some are favored for one type of shooting and some for another. Guns have specialties, just as shooters do.

Some guns are seen as cheap, others expensive. Some are traditional, others modern. Some are fast to use, some slow. As with most things to do with shotguns, however, every such statement ends with the word "but ... ." There are exceptions to everything. The single-shot shotgun can be the cheapest (and most cheaply made) gun imaginable, yet some beautiful and

This is an Ithaca Single-Barrel Trap Gun, circa 1921, the most famous and longest lived of the American single-barreled trap guns. It was produced in one form or another, until 1991.

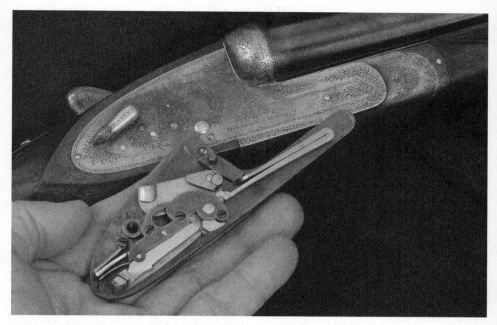

A Holland & Holland side-by-side with detachable sidelocks. This is certainly at the higher end of the cost spectrum.

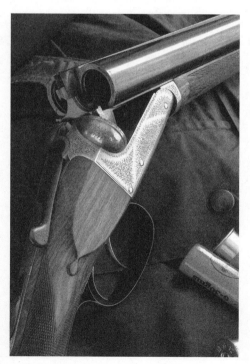

The famous Anson & Deeley boxlock, as used by P. Webley to create this classic English double.

very expensive trap guns are single-shots. Similarly, you can buy a knockabout side-by-side for $500, or spend $100,000 for a custom-built English gun.

Of the new guns you see at a shooting range today, the majority are either semi-automatics or over/unders, and either of these is a fine choice for an all-around gun. The side-by-side, once the dominant design throughout the world, has become largely a niche gun, displaced by over/unders in many applications, and America's traditional favorite, the pump gun, is being increasingly crowded out by semi-autos.

SINGLE-SHOTS

The typical "farm boy" gun is a single-barreled single-shot that is hinged at the breech and breaks open for loading. In days gone by, many different makers produced such guns, and these firearms sold for a few dollars. They were inexpensive, simple to make, reliable in operation, and durable to a fault. They could be found in all gauges, in different barrel lengths, and with varying degrees of choke. Generally, such guns are light for their gauge, which means they kick like a mule, but, for a gun to keep behind the henhouse door, they were quite acceptable.

At the other end of the single-shot scale is the expensive trap gun. Trapshooting is a sport of breaking clay pigeons, a game that grew out of the original live-pigeon shooting, in which birds were released from actual traps. Betting was heavy in that sport, prize money was big, and serious trap shooters were prepared to pay a high price for a gun that helped them win. Out of this grew the single-barrel trap gun, highly refined and beautifully made. These were manufactured by every high-end gun maker in the world, from Italy to England to the United States. Here, the most famous (and the longest lived) was the Ithaca.

The demands on a single-shot are very simple. There is no need for selective ejection, and most trap guns do not have a safety. For this reason, gun makers can and have been very fanciful in their designs. The most far-out of all time was the Ljutic Space Gun, marketed in the 1980s. It threw out every theory of fit and shootability, and the result was a gun that looked like a crowbar with handles, but, by all accounts, shot quite well. Today, Ljutic makes a more conventional drop-down single-shot with a frame that resembles a modern semi-auto. There are other small trap gun makers still in business in the United States, and their guns typically sell in the range of $8,000 to $20,000.

Having said this about single-shots, there really isn't much else to say. They are still made, although not in such great numbers as before, and the cheap models are exclusively utility guns. As for trap shooters, today they are more likely to go to the range with a good Italian over/under, since those

The futuristic receiver of the Browning Cynergy over/under.

are also usable for the game of doubles trap and can be fitted with a separate single barrel if that configuration is preferred.

Single-shot guns have also been built on other actions, such as the W.W. Greener using the Martini-Henry, and there are some single-shot bolt-actions. These are rarely seen and no longer made. Some single-shot guns were even built on converted Mauser K98 military actions, but these were utilitarian, at best.

SIDE-BY-SIDE DOUBLES

The side-by-side shotgun occupies a unique place in history, being directly descended from the flintlock and with an ancestry that stretches back centuries. The side-by-side was perfected before any of the other major styles were thought of and, for many years, it was the dominant gun in every country that made or used shotguns.

The over/under, pump, and semi-auto

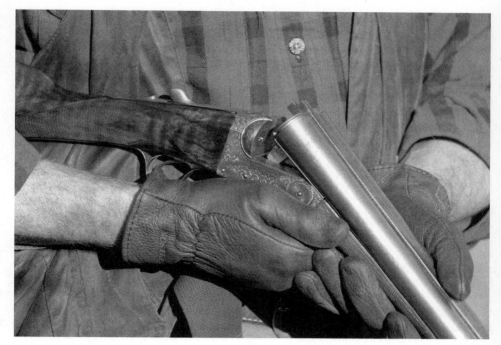

When carried "broken," a double gun (either side-by-side or over/under), is seen to be safe even at a distance.

were not designed to improve on the side-by-side, so much as to allow mass production, reduced costs and, to a limited extent, increase firepower. (This last requirement is largely negated in wild game shooting today, with most jurisdictions having a capacity limit of three shots.) The major strike against the side-by-side today is that its unquestioned virtues—light weight, exquisite balance, and a mechanism that performs flawlessly and effortlessly—can only be achieved with a great deal of highly skilled hand labor.

As the name implies, the side-by-side has two barrels aligned horizontally. Like the single-shot, it is hinged at the breech and breaks open for loading. A century ago, the side-by-side was the preferred gun of serious shotgunners, and the very best ones were made in London, by makers such as Holland & Holland, Purdey, and Boss. Fine side-by-sides were (and are) also made in

Belgium, Italy, Germany, and Spain. European shotguns of this type were intended primarily for shooting driven game—birds that are flushed over a line of waiting guns by a group of beaters. Holland & Holland and Purdey are still in business, in London, and will make you a custom shotgun for $80,000 to $100,000. It will have the finest workmanship, inside and out, with a stock carved from stunning walnut, extensive engraving, and fit and finish second to none.

In the United States, famous names in double guns included Parker, Fox, Ithaca, L.C. Smith, and Winchester. Most of the great double-gun makers went under around the time of the Great Depression or just after the Second World War, driven out of business by rising costs and changing tastes. The undoubted virtues of a good double could not compete with the one overriding virtue of a pump gun: low cost.

Side-by-side doubles are light and carry comfortably either open or on the shoulder.

What are the advantages of a double? A traditional side-by-side, made to measure, offers exquisite balance combined with the weight and gauge desired and an instant choice of chokes from two barrels. Beyond that, arguments abound as to whether the over/under is better than the side-by-side, for whatever purpose, or whether you are really better off with a pump or semi-auto.

Much of this boils down to nothing more than individual taste, with everyone having biases and preferences. Generally, however, many expert shooters have concluded that the side-by-side has an edge, when it comes to reacting to the unexpected, as in wild-game shooting, while the over/under has an advantage shooting predictable targets, such as those found in trap or skeet.

Any break-action gun has one undeniable advantage, and that is safety. When the gun is broken, not only can it not be fired, it can also be seen to be safe from

a distance. This is very desirable when shooting in a group, whether it is driven grouse in Scotland, or in a party of pheasant hunters in the Dakotas.

Another advantage of the double is its silent operation. A side-by-side double with extractors can be opened, loaded, closed, and pointed at a target in near absolute silence. It can also be opened and unloaded without making a sound, or carried open over the arm (and absolutely safe), then be closed and ready to fire in an instant, with almost no noise at all. This can be critical in hunting wary birds such as wild turkeys, and is even useful to avoid spooking well-educated, late-season pheasants.

Modern side-by-sides are divided into two main types, the sidelock and the boxlock. Of the two, the sidelock is the more aristocratic action, and certainly more expensive. There are both historical and technical reasons for this, and while

The Galazan RBL, a modern boxlock side-by-side based on the English Anson & Deeley action and manufactured by the Connecticut Shotgun Manufacturing Company.

the arguments have raged for almost 150 years as to which is better, the consensus is that the sidelock is superior overall by a number of measures. At the same time, it costs as much to produce an ultra-fine boxlock as it does a comparable sidelock. But most buyers are unwilling to pay as much for a boxlock as for a sidelock—or, to put it another way, if they are going to spend big money, they might as well get a sidelock. In modern terms, most "affordable" guns are boxlocks, while the "fine" guns are sidelocks.

The sidelock is directly descended from the hammer gun. The only real difference is that a sidelock has its tumblers (hammers) on the inside of the lock plate, while the hammer gun has them on the outside. These lock plates can be readily removed for cleaning and adjustment. The plates themselves afford more metal surface for elaborate engraving, although that is strict-

ly a secondary consideration, a side effect rather than cause. The Holland & Holland, Purdey, Boss, and Woodward actions, the most famous names in London gun making, all are sidelocks.

The London connection played no small part in the sidelock's aristocratic image. When the centerfire cartridge was developed, in the 1860s, it became apparent to a number of English gun makers (and we are concentrating on England, because that is where the major developments took place), that there was really no need for conventional hammers at all. The first really successful attempt at a so-called "hammerless" design was by a gun maker named Theophilus Murcott. It was patented in 1871. I say so-called, because all side-by-sides have hammers, it's just that some are internal and others external.

Murcott was from London, the home of the "bespoke" or custom-made, high-

The detachable lock of the Galazan A-10 sidelock over/under.

quality shotgun. In England, there were also military and mass-production gun makers, mostly in the industrial city of Birmingham. There was a great rivalry between London and Birmingham, a fact that played a prominent part in the relative images of sidelocks and boxlocks.

One of the preeminent Birmingham firms, then as now, was Westley Richards. In 1875, two Westley Richards employees, William Anson and John Deeley, patented one of the most famous inventions of all time: patent #1756, the Anson & Deeley boxlock action. In this design, the entire lock mechanism was placed inside the gun's frame. It was then given the name "boxlock," because of the square, boxy appearance of the action. Since 1875, the Anson & Deeley action has been produced in the tens of millions and is by far the most common—and still the finest— boxlock action in existence. Westley Rich-

ards naturally specialized in boxlocks, thanks to its two employees, and the boxlock became associated with working-class Birmingham, while the sidelock held sway in aristocratic London.

That, of course, oversimplifies by a wide margin. Sidelocks were also made in Birmingham, and boxlocks in London, some good and some better in either case. Broadly speaking, the modern sidelock, in its perfected form, is slightly stronger than a boxlock, has a better trigger pull, and is, theoretically, safer, because it is fitted with a secondary safety sear. This is a mechanism to catch the tumbler if it is accidentally jarred loose. The standard Anson & Deeley has no safety sear, although the conventional safety mechanisms found on both types are essentially the same.

Another feature found on some sidelocks is the "self-opener." This is an inte-

The Galazan A-10 sporting gun is equipped with auxiliary weights, for adjusting balance.

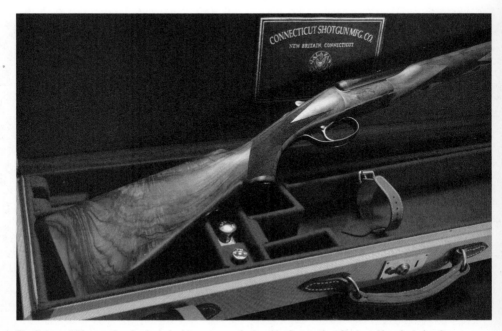

The Galazan RBL, a modern boxlock double gun, manufactured by Connecticut Shotgun Manufacturing Co.

The author hunting quail in Alabama, shooting a Charles Lancaster sidelock double, circa 1907. Photo by J. Guthrie

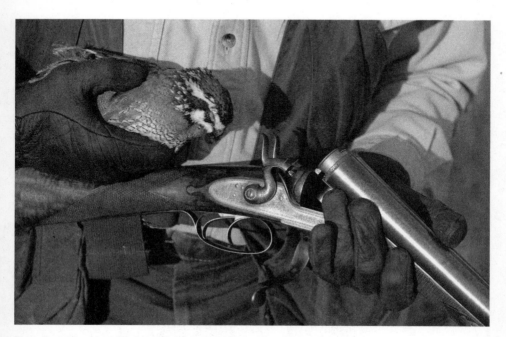

The author with a James Woodward hammer gun and bobwhite quail. Photo by J. Guthrie

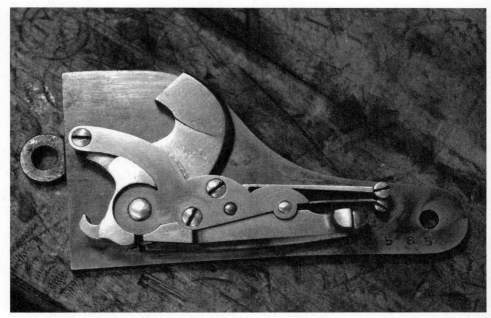

A lock plate from a Charles Lancaster sidelock. The tumbler, spring, and related mechanism are all fastened to the plate, which can be removed for cleaning and adjustment.

gral part of the Purdey action (designed by Frederick Beesley), as well as Beesley's later patent, which was manufactured largely by Charles Lancaster. Holland & Holland developed a self-opening mechanism that is standard on its Royal. A self-opener uses spring power to assist in opening the gun and allow faster loading, but it is more than a convenience. A gun with a self-opener lasts longer, because the constant tension applied to the action reduces wear from jarring and recoil. This is one reason for the legendary durability of Purdey guns. While self-openers such as the separate H&H design can be fitted to boxlocks, it is not common any more than the fitting of safety sears.

If one can apply a general rule to sidelocks and boxlocks, it is this: A good boxlock is better than a mediocre sidelock, because the advantages of either, slight to begin with, depend to a great extent on the quality of the workmanship. Some very poor sidelocks have been produced, as have some extraordinarily fine boxlocks.

In America, the high-quality side-by-sides were, with one major exception, boxlocks, although none were built on the Anson & Deeley design. The hammerless Parker, Fox, Ithaca, and Winchester 21 were all boxlocks; only the L.C. Smith was a sidelock. The Smith sidelock lacks a safety sear and is, by English standards, a rather crude and inelegant mechanism overall. The other designs came about largely from a desire to circumvent the Anson & Deeley patent.

If the "not invented here" bias affected the exchange of technology between London and Birmingham, it was an even greater factor in relations between England and America. Through the 1870s, America's demand for high-quality shotguns was filled largely by English companies, notably W&C Scott and Sons, and W.W. Greener, both of Birmingham.

Exporting to the U.S. was a major source of revenue, and patents were filed and enforced on both sides of the Atlantic. American gun makers sprang up to compete with the English guns that had such a sterling reputation, and patent infringement or the paying of licensing fees was a significant concern.

It is sometimes forgotten that there was a great deal of back and forth between the English and American gun trades through the mid-1800s, from Samuel Colt and the revolver to Greener supplying shotguns to Wells Fargo. Industrialists visited each others' factories and studied methods and designs; at one point, the English purchased American gun making machinery to modernize their own production. No wonder the design and production of side-by-side guns in the two countries are so closely related!

In the 1980s, as interest in double guns revived, attempts were made to resurrect some of the best of the old names. The Parker Reproduction was manufactured in Japan, and, later, Galazan began making the A.H. Fox guns once again. Ithaca also came back, in a short-lived venture called Ithaca Classic Doubles. For years, the only surviving original was the Winchester 21. As Winchester went through cycles of corporate financial grief, the 21 hung on by its teeth, retained purely as a prestige item.

While the English double gun survives in both London and Birmingham, the American double survives in Connecticut, with Tony Galazan's Connecticut Shotgun Manufacturing Company (CSMC). The Parker, Fox, and Winchester 21 are all manufactured by CSMC, at Galazan's factory in New Britain. There he employs a hundred workers, including some of the country's most skilled craftsman, and they work with advanced, computerized machinery. Galazan also makes his own boxlock shotgun, the RBL,

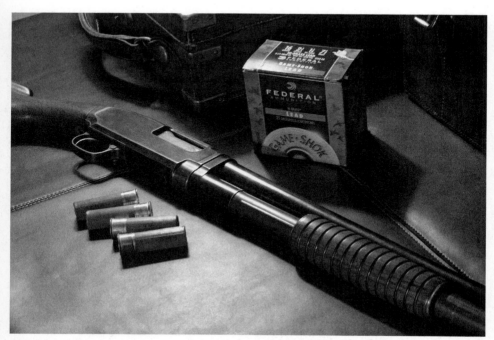

A Winchester Model 12 pump shotgun, this one in 16-gauge. The Model 12 is considered by many to be the finest pump gun ever made.

in a wide variety of configurations, from a short-barreled slug gun with rifle sights to a long-barreled, heavy sporting clays guns and everything in between.

None of these guns is cheap—far from it. You could buy 10 pump guns for the price of a new double, and while the used gun market for doubles has its ups and downs, the general, inexorable trend is up. To an extent, the double shotgun today is a prestige item. It is also a connoisseur's gun, with clubs and organizations devoted to the study and use of older guns. If you consider them in terms of a lifetime investment, these guns actually need not be expensive, a the best doubles were made to be shot a lot and last a long time.

Jack O'Connor, long-time shooting editor of *Outdoor Life*, was a great double-gun admirer and owned, among others, several Winchester 21s and five or six custom-built AYA and Eusebio Arizaga guns

from Spain. Writing in the 1960s, a time when doubles were at a low ebb, O'Connor noted their ease of handling, their light weight, the sheer joy of operating a fine mechanism, and the certain indefinable something that comes with handling a fine double. He once wrote wryly, as only he could, "The side-by-side double is seen as the 'gentleman's gun'—although I doubt that's the only requirement."

* * *

There is a distinct subdivision of the side-by-side: the hammer gun. The hammerless side-by-side as we know it today grew out of the hammer gun, which, in turn, is descended directly from pinfires, percussion guns, and flintlocks. Although the hammer gun was largely superseded by hammerless designs, starting in the 1870s, gun makers continued to produce them until the 1920s. A few are still made today.

The Ruger Red Label in 28-gauge is a light, handy game gun.

A collector's rack of Winchester Model 12 pump guns.

In the 1990s, hammer guns enjoyed a revival of interest in the United States, and prices for vintage guns shot up. Today, the peak has passed, although there is still a steady demand for hammer guns from competitors in such period-specific competitions as Cowboy Action shooting and the Order of Edwardian Gunners (known as "Vintagers"). There is also a small coterie of devotees who simply enjoy using hammer guns for both game shooting and clays.

The hammer gun has some distinct advantages even over hammerless doubles, and this is the reason they hung on long after they were obsolescent. One is that they are extremely rugged, reliable, and safe. They can be manufactured more cheaply than a hammerless gun, and tens of thousands were produced in England, for export to India, Africa, and the other colonies. The mechanism itself is considerably simpler than a hammerless gun and, therefore, less likely to malfunction; if it

does malfunction, it is easier to repair.

There is another point about hammer guns, and that is that even after the arrival of boxlocks and sidelocks, some of the finest game shooters in the world continued to favor external hammers. Both Lord Ripon (considered the best game shot the world has ever seen), and King George V (generally conceded to be one of the top four or five shots in England) used Purdey hammer guns to the end of their days.

A gun with rebounding hammers (patented by John Stanton, in England, in 1867), requires no safety mechanism and can be seen instantly to be cocked or not. As well, there is no internal cocking mechanism required. One should hasten to add that hammer guns have been made with both safeties and internal cocking mechanisms, but these are the rare exceptions.

As with any gun, using a hammer gun safely and effectively requires education and practice. Once acquired, however, fa-

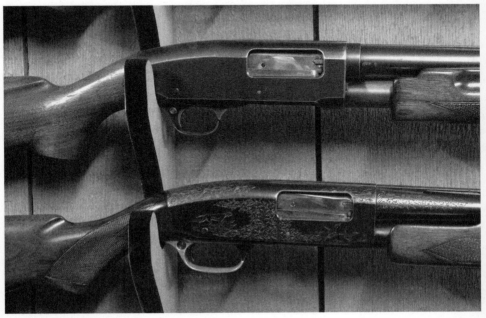

Remington Model 31 pump guns.

A Model 12 lover, this is Ralph Gates, of Missouri, with his favorite competition Model 12.

The author shooting a Winchester Model 12 (16-gauge). A pump can be operated more quickly than a semi-auto.
Photo by Ralph Gates

cility with a hammer gun becomes second nature, and many enthusiasts refuse to use anything else. They become accustomed to thumbing back one or both hammers as required, breaking the gun with the hammers cocked for safe carrying, and letting the hammers down with the gun broken, absolutely the safest method. The hammer gun offers the option of carrying a gun with rounds in the chambers and the hammers safely at half cock. Altogether, the hammer gun requires not only a few different skills, but a distinctly different attitude than a modern conventional gun of any description. In operation, it is also the quietest gun ever designed, anywhere.

OVER/UNDERS

While the over/under is usually considered more modern than the side-by-side, in fact, the first doubles were over/unders. The side-by-side became dominant largely because it was easier to configure a hammer mechanism to fire left and right barrels than it was upper and lower.

When guns went hammerless, beginning in the 1870s, makers became interested in over/under designs once again. These gained favor for a number of reasons, one of which was the fact that the shooter looking down the barrel sees only one barrel. Makers like Browning, inventor of the famous Superposed, pushed this idea until it became an article of faith.

Regardless the reasons, the over/under is, today, by far the dominant form of the modern double shotgun, with very fine ones made in England, Germany, the United States, and Italy. The over/under owns the trap, skeet, and sporting clays world and has made serious inroads with live-pigeon shooting.

It is possible to buy a Fabbri over/under from Italy, made to measure for

$200,000, or an off-the-shelf American Ruger Red Label for $2,000. There are good Italian over/unders (and some very poor ones), selling for $3,000 to $30,000 and up. In other words, there is some-thing for almost any serious shotgunner, regardless the bank account.

Like the side-by-side, the over/under has the great advantage, when used in groups of shooters, of being instantly seen

Doves in Argentina, where they are so numerous they are a serious agricultural pest, and where they are shot by the thousands. The favorite gun used by visiting shooters in the ultra-dependable Benelli 20-gauge semi-auto.

Argentine secretario Angel Mameli, a skilled loader and gun handler, keeps his Benelli 20-gauge guns functioning flawlessly through thousands of shots fired in each day.

as "safe" when broken open and carried over the arm. With two barrels, you can have two different chokes and an instant choice of which one to use. The guns can be light or heavy, depending on the use, and well balanced. Over/unders also lend themselves to having multiple barrel sets—different lengths, chokes, configurations, even different gauges—which can be fitted to the same frame. Indeed, a person desiring to own just one gun but shoot a wide variety of disciplines is better off with a good over/under than with any other type of shotgun.

The modern era of the over/under began, in 1909, when John Robertson, then the owner of Boss & Co., one of London's preeminent gun makers and designers, patented his design. Boss' great rival at the top of the London gun making tree, James Woodward & Sons, followed, in 1913, with an over/under of its own.

Prior to Boss and Woodward, one of the greatest strikes against the popularity of the over/under had been the depth required of the frame to stack two barrels atop one another, plus the lugs beneath for pivoting and room to accommodate a locking mechanism. Boss solved this by rotating the barrels on a wide radius milled into the sides of the frame, while Woodward used a system of trunnions similar to the age-old artillery pattern. Today, every modern over/under uses one or the other or a variation thereof.

The other major problem with over/unders was the extreme angles at which the strikers needed to be placed in order to be struck by conventional tumblers. This led to soft, glancing blows and chronic misfires (a problem that exists to this day, in some designs). The German company Blaser solved this on its superb, current day F3 shotgun by eliminating tumblers altogether, instead using parallel, spring-powered strikers. These strikers are tripped by a trigger mechanism that is the best in the world, one combining a perfect trigger pull with lightning-quick lock time.

Blaser was not the first to do this— Rottweil used a similar system on its short-lived over/under in the 1980s—but Blaser perfected it. The company, which employs the finest computerized machinery at its plant in Isny, in the Bavarian Alps, has also perfected the concept of complete interchangeability among parts, allowing the owner of an F3 to buy additional barrel sets, buttstocks, and fore-ends and interchange them without gunsmithing or special fitting. This is a goal that had eluded fine gun makers for more than a century. Although parts can certainly be made interchangeable, in the past, it could only be achieved by allowing excessive tolerances, which gave sloppy fits and short service lives.

The dominant competition over/under today is the Italian Perazzi, which initially made its name, in 1968, with gold medal wins at the Mexico City Olympics. Its guns have crowded the winner's circle ever since. Other great names in over/unders include Beretta, grandfather of them all, and Antonio Zoli, in Italy, as well as Krieghoff, in Germany. The Krieghoff is a German adaptation of the only great, early, American-made over/under, the Remington Model 32.

While Italian and German over/unders dominate the field, Tony Galazan's Connecticut Shotgun Manufacturing Company is fighting back with two recent models, the A-10 sidelock and the Inverness boxlock. These guns begin in the $5,000 to $10,000 range. Galazan still offers its own Galazan over/under, first produced in the early 1990s and patterned on the Boss. It is a gorgeous gun, with a price to match.

As with side-by-sides, over/unders can be made with either sidelocks or boxlock designs, although most of the so-called box-

locks are really trigger-plate mechanisms. The Woodward and Boss over/unders are both sidelocks. The original notable German design, the Merkel, uses a trigger-plate action called the "Blitz," which established a worldwide reputation.

Recognizing the need to introduce American shooters to the joys of double guns at an affordable price, in 1977, Sturm, Ruger & Company introduced the Red Label over/under. It was styled on the Boss, in appearance at least, although it is a boxlock design. Two generations of American shotgunners have made their start with Red Labels. Many have graduated to more expensive doubles, while others have seen no reason to change.

John M. Browning's last gun design was the Superposed over/under, a gun that was made in Belgium, from its beginning, in 1928, to its end, in the 1970s. With this gun, Browning undertook a marketing campaign that some describe as brilliant, others as cynical and misleading; everyone agrees it was effective. The campaign revolved around the concept of the "single sighting plane" as an alleged advantage in shooting. The idea was that, since the shooter could see only the top barrel, it is easier to aim that type of gun than it is a side-by-side. Catalog illustrations showed the single barrel alongside a double with wide, sharply defined, dark muzzles.

This campaign worked so well that the term "single sighting plane" is now chorused endlessly by proponents of single-barrel guns of all types, and many shooters who claim not to be able to shoot a side-by-side cite its lack of a "single sighting plane" as the reason. In truth, this makes no sense, for a number of reasons. First, in shooting a shotgun, you look at the target, not at the barrels. One barrel or two, the muzzle of your gun is a vague blur. Second, Browning's sharply defined illustrations were inaccurate. When you look down the barrels of a double, *even if you focus your eyes on the barrels themselves*, they almost disappear because of light reflection off the radius of the polished steel. You do see the converging lines on each side of the rib, directing your eye to a very prominent bead that stands out like the Washington Monument. This is true even if the bead itself is the tiny, discreet brass pellet favored by London gun makers. Ignore the bead (as you should), and your eye is directed naturally out to where the target is. Conversely, a broad, cross-hatched or serrated rib atop a single barrel does not direct your eye anywhere in particular.

The Perazzi MX28B, a superb new over/under 28-gauge game gun, introduced in 2012. At $14,000, this "basic" gun is not inexpensive, but it is a beautiful shooting tool.

Leaving aside the question of sighting planes, how do over/unders compare with side-by-sides in other ways?

There are two practical features to consider. One is the distance an over/under must open to allow ejection and loading. This is called the "gape," in gun making parlance, and, with an over/under, it is obviously much greater. This not only slows down the process, it can make loading awkward in confined spaces such as duck blinds, duck boats, and shooting butts. The long rotation required adds to the resistance, and it is much more difficult to make an over/under operate smoothly and effortlessly than it is a side-by-side.

The very best side-by-sides like the Holland & Holland or Purdey magnify this advantage with self-opening mechanisms or "assisted" openers. The Lancaster self-opening action, built on the 1884 Beesley patent, allows the shooter to hold two cartridges in his left hand and operate the top lever with his right thumb; the barrels spring open and eject the cartridges, two new ones are popped in, and the gun is snapped shut, ready to shoot again. No over/under is equipped with a self-opener that completely eliminates the use of the left hand to open

them, something that is an enormous advantage, when you need to reload quickly.

Then we come to the various gauges and how well they adapt to either pattern. Broadly speaking, a 12-gauge side-by-side is much more sleek and graceful than any 12-gauge over/under. The most graceful over/under is the 20-gauge and, for a considerable number of shooters, their dream gun is a finely engraved Italian 20-gauge over/under. In 28-gauge, either style can be lovely, always provided they are built on scaled-down frames and are not merely 20-gauge guns fitted with 28-gauge barrels. The same is true of the .410.

In skeet shooting, where four gauges are used in registered competition, the over/under has cornered the market. As far back as the 1960s, over/under guns were offered with four sets of barrels, one in each gauge, allowing the competitor the enormous advantage of having one gun with one familiar action and trigger pull. Today, guns like the Blaser F3 take it several steps further, balancing the smaller gauge barrels with adjustable weights so that the gun feels almost identical regardless which gauge is being shot.

This is something no side-by-side has ever done or even attempted to do (although

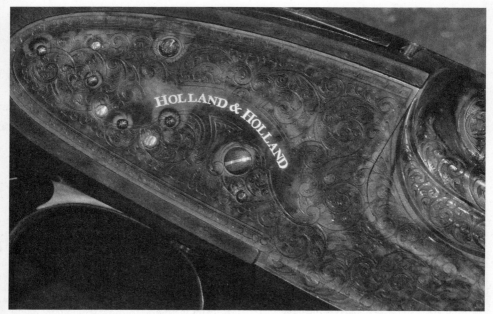

A new Holland & Holland over/under.

The trunnions that were used to elevate cannon since time immemorial were the basis for the operation of the modern over/under. The idea was first used by J. Woodward & Sons, in 1913.

multi-barrel sets are common, and sometimes in different gauges). If you are game shooting with a 28-gauge, you want it to feel like a 28-gauge, otherwise what's the point? But in competition, where weight is not an issue (and more weight is even desirable, for damping recoil), the over/under with multiple barrels wins hands down over every other type of shotgun.

In American trap, the over/under can be used with a single barrel for 16-yard shoots, and an over/under barrel for doubles, again allowing the use of just one gun for two different disciplines. This ability of the modern over/under has all but killed the traditional single-barrel trap gun, although Browning's BT-99, introduced in 1969, is still available and continues to have a loyal following.

The final point to consider with over/unders is weight. The average over/under weighs one to two pounds more than a comparable side-by-side. While a good 12-gauge English game gun weighs 6½ to

Holland & Holland over/unders incorporate its barrel selector in its safety catch. This is the most common design today.

seven pounds, it is not unusual to find an over/under game gun at eight or 8½. There are a number of reasons for this. One is that over/under buttstocks almost all have pistol grips—actually, they are bulkier in every way. They also employ a stock bolt to fasten the stock to the action, which adds ounces. The frames are heavier and fore-ends considerably bulkier, because of the need to wrap lots of wood around the barrels.

Perhaps the major reason for the additional weight of an over/under is that their makers (except for Woodward and Boss, which were catering to a different market), have never had any *need* to try to reduce weight. They never needed to shave barrel walls meticulously, by hand striking, to perfect the weight and balance. Since it is easier and cheaper to leave parts bulky, and since engineers perceive that this will reduce breakage and make them safer, many over/unders have a bulky, clumsy feel to them. Still, a 20-gauge over/under can easily be built to weigh in the neighborhood

of 6½ pounds, ideal for a gun to be carried in the field and regardless of gauge.

This largely explains the great and growing popularity of the 20-gauge over/under. Combined with a three-inch chamber and the possibility of "duplicating" 12-gauge loads via the use of three-inch magnum 20-gauge shells, on paper, you have what appears to be a perfect compromise. It isn't, of course, because no 20-gauge shotshell, regardless load and choke, can match the 12-gauge ballistically or for pattern quality. It's those immutable laws of physics again. And the magnum 20 in a gun of that weight kicks like the very devil, which is why most people stick to standard 20-gauge shotshells, except for extreme circumstances.

Overall, the over/under looks set to continue edging the side-by-side out of the picture, except in the hands of some devotees. Today, there is even a perception that the side-by-side cannot hold its own in competition and, so, there are separate

Another view of the trunions that inspired the likes of the over/under shotgun. It was first used by Boss & Co., in 1909, and a variation by J. Woodward & Sons was brought to life in 1913.

side-by-side categories set up in everything from "vintage skeet" to pigeon matches and sporting clays, just as there are small-gauge divisions.

There is also a perception that an over/under is somehow more durable than a side-by-side, and you will hear gun salesmen, trying to sell something else, condemning London side-by-sides as finicky or delicate. Nothing could be further from the truth. London guns are made to endure thousands of shots in a day, tens of thousands over a season, without malfunction and only regular cleaning and a once a year trip to the gun maker for a strip and clean. That is the reality of life in driven shooting, and Boss, Purdey, and H&H realize that very well. As an example, there is one documented case of a Boss side-by-side game gun used at the old Eley ammunition factory for routine testing. With nothing more than an occasional cleaning, the gun had fired an estimated 1.5 *million* rounds, when the factory closed down.

That is durability. It is also the reason why hundred-year-old Hollands and Woodwards are in regular use today. There is a thriving market in century-old English side-by-sides, and the interest in them is for use in the field, not for collecting or wall-hanging.

PUMP (SLIDE-ACTION) GUNS

For many years, the pump could lay claim to being the all-American gun. From the early models in the 1890s until today, every major manufacturer made one, and they were refined into guns that were handy, durable, and dependable.

Pump guns were used to win big-money trap matches, to shoot ducks and geese in rainy salt marshes, and to knock off foxes threatening the henhouse. They were used as trench guns in the Great War, and by police and prison guards. There is no use to which a shotgun can be put that the pump gun cannot handle.

Pump guns, many and varied. In the middle of a rack of Remington Model 31 game and competition guns rests an Ithaca Model 37 trench gun, identified by its quite short barrel and its ventilated cover. The versatility of the American pump gun is nearly unlimited.

The pump is a single-barreled repeater with its cartridges held in a tubular magazine under the barrel. Operated by the forward hand, the fore-end slides back and forth, using the magazine as a rail. It opens and closes the bolt, ejecting the empty hull and chambering a fresh round. Although pump guns have been made everywhere from Japan to Italy and Brazil, the design is predominantly American, as are the most famous models. These include the Winchester Model 12 (lamented in its discontinuation and highly collectible), and the current production champion, the Remington Model 870. The Model 870 replaced an earlier Remington design, the Model 31. Since 1949, the 870 has become the single most produced civilian firearm in history, with more than 10 million made by Remington and still going strong.

The third great American pump is the Ithaca Model 37. It is named for the year of its introduction, 1937, and was derived from a Remington patent of a Browning design that had expired. The Ithaca Model 37 thrived, even as Ithaca's famous double guns were losing ground, and it is still in production today. The 37 loads and ejects through the bottom of the action, allowing a solid frame that is both strong and weatherproof. Its solid mechanism feels as if it is running on ball bearings.

Like the underlever on some double guns or the mechanism on a lever-action rifle, the basic pump mechanism is both intuitive and ergonomic. For a shooter, it is a natural movement. In effect, the shooter becomes part of the mechanism, which is activated by a combination of recoil and the natural retraction of the shooter's forward hand, gripping the slide, after a shot is fired. As the slide is then pushed forward to chamber a new round, the leading hand is pushed toward the target, bringing the gun instantly into line for an accurate second shot.

This movement can be extremely fast. Tests have proven that a skilled shooter can

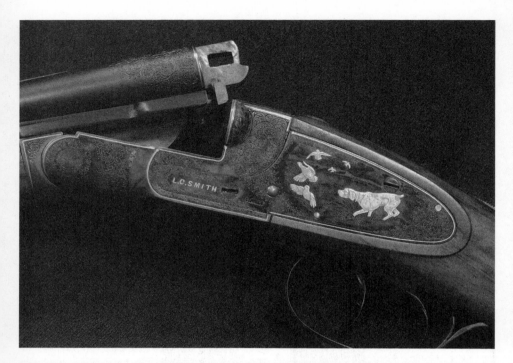

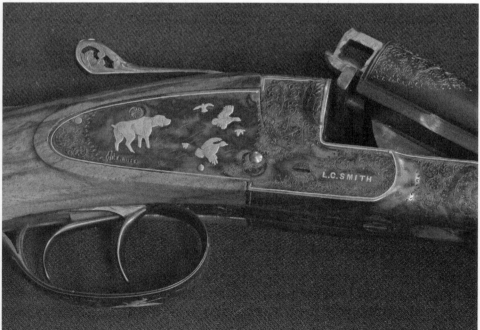

The L.C. Smith was one of very few sidelock side-by-side guns made in the United States, and the most famous. It was manufactured in some very fancy grades.

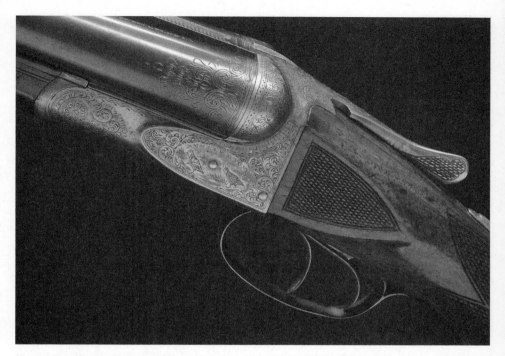

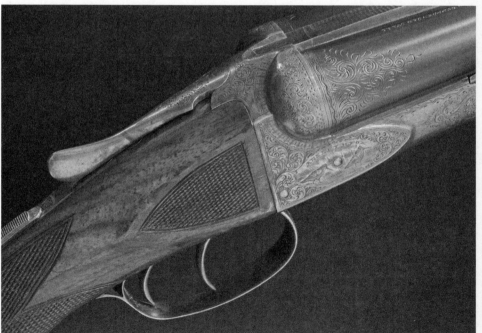

The A.H. Fox double is an American boxlock gun.

Comparing the hinge system of two of the finest English over/unders. The Woodward (top) and the Boss. Both employ the trunnions first found on cannon, and variations on this method are used on virtually all modern over/unders.

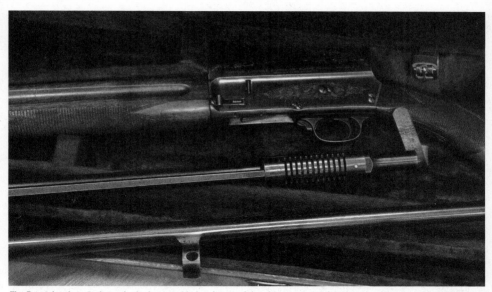

The Browning Auto-5, shown both above and below, is one of the oldest, and certainly the most famous, semi-auto designs. It was introduced in 1900, and uses a long-recoil mechanism. In operation, there is the feeling of many parts moving, but devotees love them.

fire more rounds, more quickly, from a pump gun than a semi-auto. Pumps are also simpler and more reliable, as well as extremely rugged, which makes them the ideal tactical and defense weapon.

Just as a shotgunner who grew up shooting double guns prefers them for life, so, too, do pump gunners cling to their favorites and resist any pressure to move to more sophisticated or expensive designs. The great American pump gun is still in production, led by the Remington 870 (for sales) and the Ithaca 37 (for longevity). Combined with this, there are millions and millions of good used pump guns available for just a few hundred dollars. These guns represent the greatest single bargain in the world of shooting. A person shooting a well-made Winchester Model 12 from the 1960s need make no apologies to anyone.

SEMI-AUTOMATICS

A semi-automatic shotgun is one whose mechanism functions independently of

Hand-fitting a new Winchester Model 21, at CSMC in Connecticut.

Over/under barrel sets, in progress at Connecticut Shotgun Manufacturing Company. Over/under designs lend themselves to machine production better than side-by-sides.

At CSMC, fine checkering is done by hand, but time is saved by laying out the pattern using a laser machine.

the shooter. Such an action will chamber a round, eject an empty hull, and then chamber a new round, with no overt motion required from the shooter except pulling the trigger. The power to do all this work is provided either by the force of recoil, as in the very earliest semi-automatic designs, or by utilizing expanding powder gases to push a piston rod and move the breechblock.

Although semi-automatics have been available for more than a century, they only really took hold after 1945. Since 1980, they have become the most common design found in a wide variety of applications. Semi-autos are available in every shotgun configuration, from tactical models and high-end trap guns to heavy, extra-long-chambered guns for wildfowl and turkey hunting. They are available in every modern gauge and chamber length.

Modern semi-autos, like the famous Benelli, are renowned for their durability and dependability. High-volume wingshooting operations in Central and South America, where hunters shoot thousands

Hand-filing the interior of a Francotte sidelock at CSMC.

At CSMC, every gun is taken to the range for extensive test-firing. No gun is shipped until it comes back from the range with every function perfect.

The many faces of the Benelli semi-auto, from left: a Duca di Montefeltro 20-gauge game gun, a 12-gauge M2 Tactical, and a Super Vinci 12-gauge waterfowl gun. The Super Vinci will accept up to 3½"-inch shotshells.

of doves in a day, customarily use semi-autos, with Benelli 20-gauge guns being almost the standard.

The Browning Auto-5 is one of the most famous of all semi-autos, being a John M. Browning design that was made for many years at the Fabrique National (FN) arms factory in Liège, Belgium. It was patented in 1898, production began in 1900, and it continued (discounting interruptions due to the World Wars), for almost exactly a century. The last special, commemorative guns were made by FN, in 1999. The design has been produced by several other gun makers, as well, including Remington and Franchi. The "humpback" Browning has many fans and is loved both for its dependability and pointability. However, with its square-backed receiver, it is a disconcerting gun to shoot for anyone accustomed to a double or a pump. The Auto-5 also uses a "long-recoil" design that results in a great deal of movement, to which many shoot-

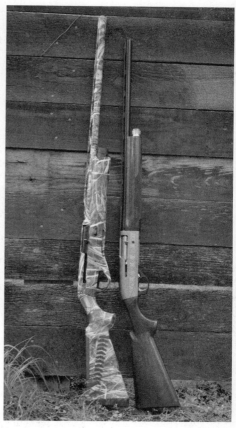

Above and left are two extremes in game guns, both by Benelli. The 20-gauge (on the left above), is a nicely appointed upland gun, while the 12-gauge Super Vinci is the latest in a camouflaged, high-powered waterfowl and turkey gun.

ers find it hard to become accustomed.

One undoubted advantage of semi-automatic shotguns is reduced recoil. The Remington 1100, introduced in 1963, was the first semi-auto to really demonstrate this. The gun has remained in production ever since and, with more than four million guns produced, is the best-selling semi-auto in history. Recoil reduction is a result of diverting some of the shotshell's energy to operate the action. For this reason, the semi-auto is often recommended for beginners, especially if a 12-gauge is needed for a particular application. A 20-gauge semi-auto, the favorite for doves in South America, has very gentle recoil, when used with standard 2¾-inch cartridges and light shot loads.

There are disadvantages. One is safety. Because the gun reloads itself almost instantly, it is always ready to fire, whether you want it to be or not. With beginners, this can be a

problem. Even the pump gun can be rendered safe, simply by pulling back the slide. With a semi-auto, the shooter needs to withdraw the breechblock and lock it in place.

In parts of the world where driven shooting of game birds is common (beaters in the fields drive flocks of birds to lines of waiting guns, those shooters usually positioned in berms), safety is a paramount concern. Many shoots prohibit semi-autos because, unlike doubles, they cannot be broken open and be seen to be safe at a distance. This practice is even followed by some pheasant-hunting operations in the Dakotas.

Trap clubs are another place that often don't welcome semi-autos because, shooting on a line, the gun flings its empty hull to one side. This can annoy the shooter next to you, if the hull bounces off him or his shotgun. Some clubs require a net over your ejection port that will catch the empties.

Finally, there are legal restrictions in some countries. Anyone travelling abroad to shoot needs to pay close attention to local laws, before attempting to import a semi-auto. Even if the gun itself is legal, there may be restrictions on magazine capacity.

MISCELLANEOUS ACTIONS

We have covered the main types of shotgun actions, but there are others. In the late 1800s, as American gun makers perfected the lever-action rifle, they tried to adapt the lever mechanism to shotguns. The same occurred with bolt-actions. In Germany, shotguns were often combined with rifle barrels in myriad designs to create multi-purpose guns.

The lever-action shotgun was an early design that lost out quickly to the pump gun. Lever shotguns were heavy, clumsy, and slow. The same was true of the bolt-action shotgun, which, in reality, was a scaled-up .22 rimfire single-shot rifle with the simplest (and one of the strongest) of mechanisms. It had its points, mainly cheapness and durability, which is why it hung on long after the lever shotgun was dead.

Several manufacturers, including Mossberg and Marlin, have made bolt-action shotguns with box magazines that hang down below the action. These are strictly utility guns and really unsuited to wingshooting.

One action that should probably have been included with either pumps or semi-autos is the combination pump/semi-auto. The most famous example is the SPAS-12, an Italian gun made by Franchi and immortalized by Arnold Schwarzenegger in *The Terminator*. The SPAS-12 has made every gun-ban wish list since 1983, largely on the image it projected in that movie. For practical use, it is heavy and clumsy.

Another real oddball is the Street Sweeper, a design that borrows from both revolvers and the old Thompson submachine gun. It originated in South Africa, and it is rarely seen in the United States,

Top and above is Ryan Mason, of Missouri, with his Beretta semi-auto competition gun decked out in the colors of the University of Missouri Tigers.

Here's Ryan again, this time with the Benelli Super Vinci, a gun with superb ergonomics to go with its futuristic appearance.

but it shows just how fanciful shotgun designs can be and how far they can stray from the original concept of a gun for shooting birds on the wing. The Street Sweeper has a short barrel and 12-round drum magazine. The drum is loaded, then powered by a wind-up spring. It rotates like a revolver cylinder and employs a double-action trigger similar to a revolver. Like the SPAS-12, it is on every gun-ban list, mostly because of its fearsome appearance and intimidating name.

* * *

Today, visiting a trap, skeet, and sporting-clays range, you might see any of the above designs in use. Each has its adherents.

In shotgunning, there are exceptions to every rule, but, generally speaking, the semi-auto has emerged as the most common all-around shotgun. Over/unders predominate in higher-level skeet, trap, and sporting clays competitions. Pump guns are found anywhere and everywhere (but rarely, these days, in the winner's circle), and side-by-sides are niche guns preferred by upland hunters or used in designated side-by-side competitions.

These divisions are not based solely, or even mostly, on what is best for a particular application. Cost plays a part, as does availability. The fact that the pump gun did not kill off the side-by-side, nor the semi-auto the pump, proves that each type of gun has enough of an edge somewhere to ensure each will be around for a long, long time.

Alison Caselman, demonstrating good form with the Benelli 20-gauge semi-auto.

CHAPTER 4

FEATURES, NICETIES, AND NUANCES

nyone browsing through a shotgun catalog today can be overwhelmed by the options available, from different grip shapes to buttstock designs, recoil pads, fore-ends, barrels, ribs, and sighting devices. On double guns, you might be offered one trigger or two and a safety that is automatic or manual. Barrels come in different lengths, with different chokes and ribs.

For the beginning shotgunner or one who is looking for an everyday, all-around gun, we can define some basics. Then, by the time you reach the point of moving on to a more expensive gun and its myriad options, you will have an idea of what you like and what you don't.

TRIGGERS

No single feature of a shotgun is so important as the trigger, in determining whether you will shoot well or badly. A gun with a poor trigger not only can give you a bad afternoon, it can upset your shooting for weeks or months to come. High-level competitors dread an encounter with a poor trigger, knowing the possible long-term effects, and many refuse ever to shoot any gun but their own for this reason.

To the uninitiated, the trigger may seem inconsequential—like discussing the operation of a car's accelerator. But, in fact, it is the critical link between the shooter's brain and the gun's mechanism. In shooting at a moving object, whether it is a wild bird or a clay pigeon, you are dealing in split-second, subconscious calculations and instinctive movement. When your brain decides that this micro-second is the point at which the shot should be fired, the signal from the brain to the finger and from the finger on the trigger to the gun's firing mechanism must be seamless and as close to instant as possible. A bad trigger, one with an unduly heavy, rough, uneven, or inconsistent pull, is an obstacle to this Zen-like flow of intent.

So, exactly what is a good trigger pull on a shotgun? Unlike rifle shooting, where the trigger is gently squeezed, a shotgun trigger is given what is sometimes described as a controlled slap. Weight of pull is measured in pounds, and the ideal is half the weight of the gun or slightly more. Thus, a seven-pound gun should have a trigger pull of about 3½ pounds. If it is a double-trigger gun, the rear trigger should be about a quarter-pound heavier than the front.

Pull weight is critical because, if you have a seven-pound gun with a nine-pound pull, the effort to trip the trigger can pull the gun off the path of the target. Such a heavy trigger is a terrible distraction, one that will cause you to slow or stop your swing and miss the target.

Just as important as weight is the quality of the pull. There should be no discernible creep or grating movement before the hammer trips. One famous description of the perfect feel is that it is like a glass rod breaking.

Double guns can have one trigger or two: singles, pumps, and semi-autos, obviously, only one. The finest triggers found today are on over/under competition guns and, of these, the trigger of Blaser's F3 shotgun is widely regarded as the very best available. Individual shotgun features can rarely be discussed in isolation; the overall quality of Blaser's firing mechanism is dependent on its unique striker design and fast lock time (the fraction of a second between the pulling of the trigger and firing of the shotshell). You might think this would be of interest only to competitors at the highest levels, but it affects everyone who shoots a shotgun and wants to hit their targets consistently.

When you move from an adequate trigger to a very fine one, like the Blaser F3, you rarely say, "This is so much better!" Instead, when you return to your old trigger you think, "Omigosh, this is *awful*!" Using a really good trigger spoils you for all the rest.

This is not to say that the triggers on a century-old Holland & Holland game gun cannot be adjusted to near perfection, because they can. Such an operation, however, requires the attention of a highly skilled gun maker. It is also not to say that you cannot become accustomed to a mediocre trigger and do reasonably well with it. Certainly, you can, but tolerating a truly poor trigger handicaps you.

With modern competition guns, trigger groups are often self-contained modules that can be adjusted only by a factory-trained technician using special tools and magnifiers to set the contact point between trigger and sear. Having a detachable trigger group such as that found on the renowned Perazzi competition over/unders

is an advantage, because it allows you to keep a spare trigger, ready to install should something go amiss in the midst of a match.

Double triggers are traditional on double shotguns and have several advantages. First, they give two independent mechanisms—in effect, two guns in one. If one malfunctions, you still have the other. Second, they allow an instant choice of left or right barrel (top or bottom, on an over/under), and that gives you an instant choice of choke and load. Double triggers are also vastly simpler than single triggers and, therefore, less prone to problems. They can be finely adjusted and are extremely reliable.

Many people consider double triggers old-fashioned or the mark of a less expensive gun. Neither is true any more than it is true to say that a standard transmission is the mark of a cheap car. Just as many drivers of expensive cars prefer a stick shift for the additional control, so do many excellent shots—including the best game shots—prefer double triggers.

Single triggers aren't actually that much newer than double triggers. They have been attempted in some form or other for several hundred years, but only when they were perfected in the 1890s did they begin to gain adherents. There are two types of single triggers, selective and non-selective.

As the name suggests, a selective trigger allows you to choose which barrel to shoot first, while a non-selective trigger simply fires the two barrels in the same order every time. A non-selective trigger is usually set up to perform right to left in the case of a standard side-by-side game gun, where the right barrel generally has the more open choke, following the assumption that flushing game is, obviously, closer for the first shot than it would be for a second shot after a miss.

The great obstacle to developing a usable single trigger, which was not understood until the 1890s, was that there is an

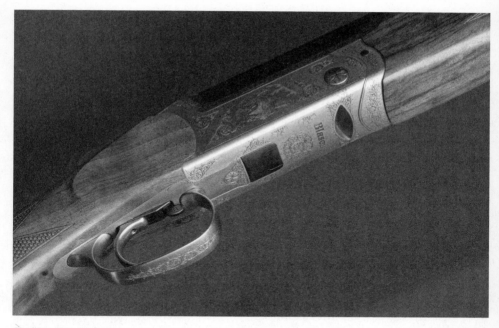

The Blaser F3's single-trigger mechanism is one of, if not the best competition triggers in the world. The barrel selector is inside the trigger guard forward of the trigger (plainly seen as the little oval tab just behind the front of the trigger guard bow in the left-hand photo). Positioned as it is, it is readily accessible, yet out of the way. The trigger on the F3 can also be moved back and forth, accommodating minor length of pull adjustments.

unconscious, involuntary second pull that occurs right after the trigger is deliberately pulled the first time. No one knows exactly why this occurs, but it does. Designers had to find a way to absorb that involuntary pull without it firing the second barrel. Various methods were employed, including "three-pull" mechanism triggers that used a pendulum or spring-loaded device to absorb the involuntary pull before positioning the trigger for the second deliberate pull.

Another consideration with single triggers is the means of setting the trigger to fire the second barrel. Some "inertia" systems rely on recoil, which means that, if your first cartridge misfires, you have no second shot, because there hasn't been any recoil—the required inertia—to reset the mechanism to fire the second barrel. Other systems set the trigger for the second barrel mechanically. Regardless, it should be plain that such

triggers are complicated in their design and functionality, and this complexity is increased if you add a selective feature that allows you to choose which barrel to fire first.

This complexity can spill over into other vital functions, such as the safety. Many selective trigger mechanisms combine the selector in the sliding safety catch on the tang, and the two positions are marked "O" and "U" (or "R" and "L," in a side-by-side) or indicated by one red dot (for the lower barrel) and two (for the upper) to fire first. Unfortunately, in the act of sliding the safety forward, the catch can inadvertently be switched to the other barrel, sometimes even left in between the two, in which case the gun may not fire at all. For this reason, many competition guns include a feature for locking the selector in position by means of a set screw. In a departure from these commonly encountered designs, the Blaser F3 has its se-

Blaser gunsmith Andre Gorjup adjusting the trigger let-off on an F3, using a magnifying and measuring device that adjusts to thousands of an inch.

The Blaser F3 trigger is a finely machined and intricate mechanism, whose principles can be traced to the first successful single triggers patented in the 1890s.

lection lever in the trigger guard, forward of the trigger itself, where it is easily accessible, but protected from accidental movement.

Here we come to a question that sparks debates at any shooting club. It is argued that a selective single trigger gives the same instant choice of barrel as double triggers do. The question is, is it really possible, in the heat of the moment and facing an unexpected situation, to do just that? In theory, the answer is unequivocally "Yes." In practice, it is an unequivocal "Unlikely."

After more than a century of regular use of selective single triggers, a few truths have emerged. In the traditional English game gun configuration of barrels and triggers, a side-by-side's right barrel is the more open choke and is fired with the forward, or right-hand, trigger. This favors right-handed people, who are in the majority.

Perhaps because our hands and eyes are horizontal and defined by left and right,

shooters have no difficulty, when assessing a situation such as a bird that appears suddenly, discerning whether to use the right or left barrel (open or tight choke) and connecting that decision with the appropriate trigger. It is intuitive, spontaneous, instant. However, if you transfer the moment of decision from "Which trigger?" to "Which barrel selector position?" a step is added that derails the process. It isn't so bad if the selector is on a side-by-side; push it left, it selects the left barrel and vice versa. Still, it's an instant's delay, and having selected the barrel, you then have to push the safety forward in order to shoot. Overall, though, it is not bad.

With an over/under, there is no such intuitive connection. Nor is there a traditional configuration with over/unders in which the bottom barrel is always one choke or the other. You always find yourself moving a tiny mechanism left or right, choosing

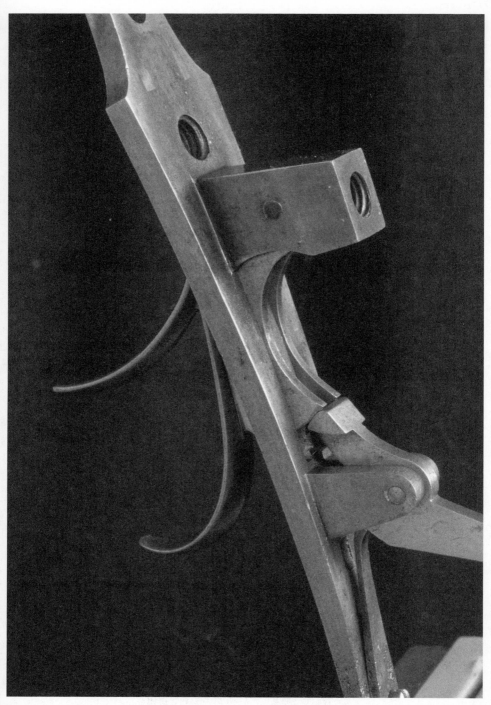

A two-trigger mechanism on an English double, circa 1890. Double triggers are simple, sturdy, and foolproof. The safety mechanism, which locks the triggers, can be clearly seen.

between up or down. For this reason, the vast majority of shooters with over/unders having selective single triggers set them to fire the bottom barrel first and leave it at that.

In this era of nearly universal interchangeable choke tubes, the problem, rather than being simplified, is magnified in its complexity, because the shooter must remember which choke he has in which barrel and then decide which he wants to use, and *then* remember which way the selector needs to be pointed in order to shoot that barrel. By this time, of course, that pheasant is in the next county, cackling all the way. In the old fixed-choke, two-trigger approach, it was simple: Long bird, back trigger; short bird, right trigger.

For some reason, double triggers are one of two shotgun features (the other being the automatic safety), that drive American gun writers to paroxysms of fury. Both have been described as "instruments of the devil" by such luminaries as Jack O'Connor. O'Connor hated double triggers, with a passion. More than once he wrote about acquiring a fine European side-by-side and having its double triggers replaced by a single trigger.

Some Americans insist they cannot use double triggers and go on at great length about the difficulties, usually blaming their problem on the fact that they did not grow up with them. I tend to view these claims with a skeptical eye. I never laid eyes on a double-triggered gun until I was in my late teens, but I took to it with no problem and have been shooting single- and double-triggered guns interchangeably ever since. The late Michael McIntosh, who knew as much about shotgun triggers as any writer in America, equally had no difficulty using one or the other, back and forth, occasionally switching several times in the course of a day.

In the same vein, some people (often the same ones!) say they cannot shoot a side-by-side, because it does not have the single sighting plane of an over/under or pump. The "single sighting plane" dodge, as I've said, was a brilliant marketing ploy originated by John M. Browning, when he introduced the Superposed over/under and wanted to seduce Americans away from their side-by-side Parkers and Ithacas. Seductive it may be, but it does not stand up to scrutiny.

First of all, every gun, regardless of the number of barrels or their configuration, has a single plane down which you look. Second, when you look down the barrels of a side-by-side, you don't see two barrels the way they are illustrated in cartoons. What you see, predominantly, are the rib and bead; reflected light turns the barrels into ill-defined ghosts. Finally, in shooting, you are not looking primarily at the barrels— you *should* be looking at the target! If you do look at the barrels, you will slow your swing and pull the trigger for a miss. The barrels should only be seen out of the figurative corner of your eye, with your attention concentrated almost laser-like on your moving target.

But I digress. As I said, rarely can one feature of a shotgun be discussed in isolation. Regardless whether they originate in a valid complaint, these are real considerations with triggers, and gun designers have gone to great lengths to address them.

For example, a separate but related concern with triggers is the dreaded flinch, a malady to which trap shooters, especially, are prone and go to great lengths to avoid. A flinch is caused by recoil, muzzle blast, or a combination of the two and manifests itself in several ways. Riflemen who suffer from a flinch jerk the trigger; some even turn and look away at the moment of firing. Shotgunners find themselves either unable to pull the trigger or involuntarily freezing

A Galazan A-10 American, in its competition guise, has a quite steep, hand-filling pistol grip.

for an instant before doing so. Invariably, both result in a miss.

Trap shooters are prone to flinching because of the sheer number of rounds they fire in a day, multiplied by months and years and tens of thousands of rounds. The effect of recoil is cumulative, and even if you are firing the lightest loads possible, as trap shooters do, there is a long-term effect.

One answer is the "release" trigger. Instead of pulling the trigger to fire the gun, you pull the trigger and then release it to fire. For many trap shooters, the release trigger has been a salvation. Obviously, such devices can only be used on competition guns, and guns with release triggers should be outfitted with loud warning stickers.

Double triggers, too, have their share of variations. Val Browning, son of John M., designed a "double-single" trigger mechanism, in which there were two triggers. Instead of moving from one to the other, however, both triggers fire both barrels, but in reverse order. If you want to fire "right-left," you pull the front trigger. If you want "left-right," you pull the other. For a while, this was offered as an option on various European side-by-sides.

Another bizarre variation was a gun in which the front and rear triggers could be

pulled in the normal order to fire right-left, but, if the rear trigger was pulled first, it fired both barrels simultaneously. This was intended for French market gunners and was often installed on guns in which the two barrels were aligned to put their patterns adjacent to each other. This spreads the shot wider than does conventional barrel regulation ("regulation" refers to how close to the same point of impact two barrels in a double-barrel gun will shoot), in which the patterns overlay one another. The wider pattern was useful for shooting at a flock of ducks rising from the water, or pigeons out of a grain field.

Such was the world of European gun making that a skilled gun maker (such as Ignacio Ugartechea, who made the gun just described), could modify triggers to perform in any way the customer wanted. If you buy a used gun and find it always doubles with the back trigger, it could well be intentional!

GRIPS

The grip, or "wrist," is the part of the stock directly behind the trigger guard that you clasp with your trigger hand. Shotguns are available with three different grip

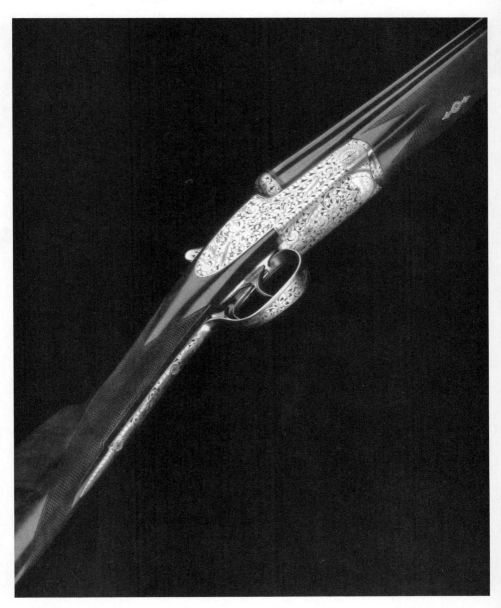

A deluxe side-by-side by AYA, one of Spain's finest gun makers, with the traditional straight, or English, grip. Such a gun is both graceful and fast.

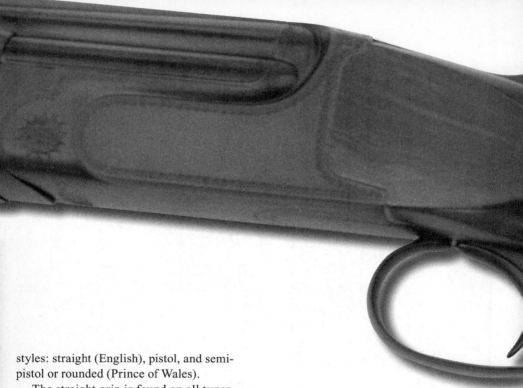

styles: straight (English), pistol, and semi-pistol or rounded (Prince of Wales).

The straight grip is found on all types of shotguns, but is typically associated with the English game gun. It is generally preferred for guns with two triggers, and the usual explanation for this is that you slide your hand back in order to pull the rear trigger. This sounds logical, but isn't true. When using a double-trigger gun, only your trigger finger moves to pull the second trigger. What the straight grip does is keep your trigger hand more closely aligned with the barrels and your lead hand on the forearm, making it more natural to point instinctively at your target. Because straight grips are slimmer, you do not hold them as tightly as you would a pistol grip.

Pistol grips are found on all competition guns, and many competitors prefer them because they can clasp them very firmly. They also position the trigger hand slightly lower. Because of the depth of the fore-end on over/unders, pump guns and semi-autos, the forward hand is also positioned lower, so, on such guns, a pistol grip better aligns the two hands.

The semi-pistol grip lies in between the two, having a more gradual curve than the pistol grip. It is usually rounded off and appears without a grip cap. This design of this grip dates to the days of hammer guns, but it became popular again around 1900, because the Prince of Wales liked it. It is also known as the "King George V" grip. Oddly enough, in Germany and Austria today, the term "Prince of Wales" is being applied to the standard, sharply curved pistol grip. The perils of arcane terminology!

Which grip you favor is almost entirely a matter of personal preference, with very little relevance to utility or efficiency. Many admirers of straight grips (this author among them), insist they are faster to bring into position when a bird flushes unexpectedly. They give a gun more graceful lines, and that translates into graceful handling. A straight grip also saves an ounce or two of weight.

A more gradual pistol grip, such as the one found on this 28-gauge Perazzi MX28B game gun, is faster for a field gun.

SAFETIES

The safety is the mechanism on a shotgun that locks the trigger, tumbler, or striker from inadvertently tripping and firing the gun. Some guns have only a trigger-block safety. Others have a secondary safety that catches the tumbler if it is jarred off the sear without the trigger having been pulled.

Safeties have been made in so many shapes, sizes, and configurations that there is not enough space in one book to cover them all. Between 1870 and 1890, the heyday of hammerless gun development in England, gun makers and inventors filed 108 patents for different safety designs. The one that emerged triumphant was the trigger-blocking safety that has the catch mounted on the top strap, just behind the toplever. There, it is easily pushed to the "Off" position by the thumb of the trigger hand, as the gun is mounted to the shoulder. This is the position found on virtually every side-by-side and over/under double gun produced today, as well as the vast majority of those made since 1880.

Guns with external hammers do not typically have a safety; the hammers' half-cock position is the normal, safe carry

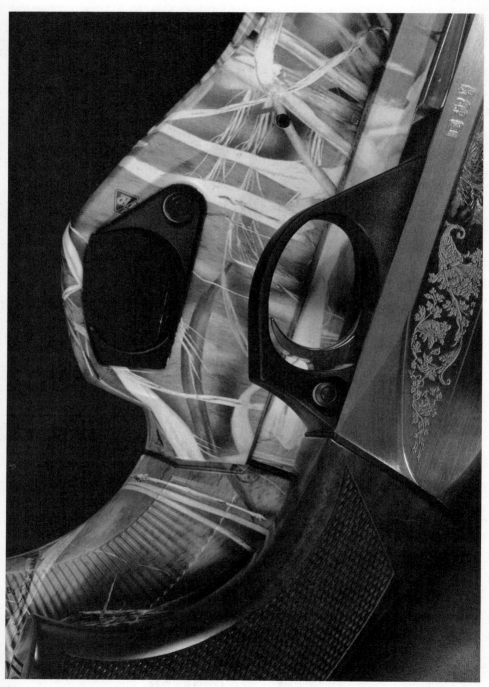

On pumps and semi-autos, safety catches are usually either behind the trigger or ahead of it. These Benelli semi-autos employ both, and both work very well.

The tang safety is almost universal with doubles of all types. It has been around a long time: the Woodward (right) was made, in 1881, in London, and the Grulla (left), in Spain, in 2002.

position. Pump guns and semi-autos usually have a button safety that moves from side to side, located either at the front or rear of the trigger guard. A button at the rear of the guard, pushed by the trigger finger, is almost as convenient as a tang safety.

Before going further, we should state very clearly that any safety device is fallible. Just because the safety is on doesn't mean a gun can be handled in an unsafe manner. Having said that, safeties do have an important role to play in shooting, and the unconscious, instinctive, automatic use of a gun's safety is an important skill for any shotgunner to acquire. The *only* time the safety on a shotgun should be off is when the gun is at the shoulder, about to fire.

One important difference found on English guns compared to modern American guns is the "automatic" safety. With such a safety, the catch is automatically pushed to "On" as the toplever is moved to open the gun. This is done by a cam on the lever spindle pushing a rod that moves the safety back.

The automatic safety became a standard feature of English guns, during the era of driven shooting and its multiple guns and loaders. During heavy action, with guns being opened, loaded, closed, and passed back and forth between loader and shooter, having the gun automatically on safe when it was opened meant that the triggers were blocked when the gun was closed, eliminating, or at least reducing, the possibility of an accidental discharge upon closing. As shooting is taught in English shooting schools to this day, the safety is pushed off with the thumb *as the gun is being mounted to the shoulder* and *never* at any other time. With practice, this becomes so instinctive that any other action is foreign and disconcerting.

Although normally ascribed to the English, the practice was once common in America. In *The Old Man and the Boy*, Robert Ruark's younger self is taught to

The Galazan A-10 American safety catch incorporates the barrel selector in its mechanism and functionality. This is the most common approach on the majority of modern over/under shotguns.

handle his first gun exactly in this way by the Old Man, complete with a demonstration and lecture.

Automatic safeties are found on all the old American doubles, though Ithaca came up with a wrinkle to this that accommodated both preferences, with a three-position safety. When pushed forward to "Off," it was returned to "On" automatically. When pulled to the rear, the safety was off and stayed off, until the shooter chose otherwise. Today's Ruger Red Label over/under, the gun that made doubles affordable for the masses, has an automatic safety, but it's easily disabled if you don't like it.

Like double triggers, the automatic safety has become an object of hatred by some American shotgunners, who remonstrate against it long and loud. Silly, really, because, if you don't like it, you can always have a gunsmith disconnect it and use the safety manually (the reverse is not true).

Early on, I mentioned secondary safeties. These are found only on sidelock shotguns (though not all), and a few high-quality boxlocks. The L.C. Smith, the classic American sidelock, did not have a secondary safety. The question is not really how effective these are, but how relatively unsafe guns without them might be. The Anson & Deeley boxlock, one of the most widely produced mechanisms in industrial history (not just gun history), does not have a secondary safety, and it is not considered an issue.

Traditionally, single-barrel trap guns are unequipped with any safety at all, simply because they are never loaded until you are about to shoot and are carried open at all other times. Newer trap guns intended to serve a multitude of uses often have the facility of locking the safety into the "Off" position. This is to ensure you never inadvertently call "pull" with the safety on and lose the bird.

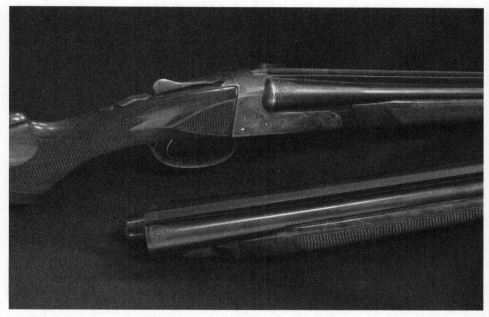

The legendary American Ithaca double had a unique safety catch with three positions, allowing the shooter to use it as either an automatic or manual safety.

Shotgun safeties definitely have a place, and using the safety, no matter where it is placed, should become second nature for every shotgunner. As well, whenever the gun is unloaded, every shooter should get into the habit of carrying a double gun broken, a pump gun with the slide back and the action open, and a semi-auto with the action locked open. This shows people, even at a distance, that the gun cannot be fired. Carrying a gun—any gun—with the safety off, while walking through brush or long grass and moving in on a bird dog's point, is certifiably dangerous.

Safety warnings on even the most innocuous of products have become so pervasive in modern society that people either ignore them or forget them within minutes. But, with shotguns, the safety and the use thereof is an integral part of using the gun properly. Like Robert Ruark and the Old Man, their use should be taught

early, insisted upon always, and transgressions punished without mercy. A safety should never be regarded as an absolute safeguard, but it should always be on when the gun is loaded and not about to be fired. Period. End of story.

CHOKES

"Choke" is the constriction at the shotgun muzzle that regulates how much the pellets spread to form a pattern downrange. It can best be likened to the nozzle of a hose, adjusted to give a wide or narrow spray. Also as it is with a hose, when the spray is widened, the range becomes shorter; when the stream of water is concentrated, it shoots farther, but covers a smaller area, and it becomes more difficult to hit anything.

Although choke was first patented by William Rochester Pape, in England, in

This is a two-barrel set for a modern trap gun, specifically, this one a Browning Cynergy. There is an "un-single" for 16-yard trap and over/under barrels for doubles trap. Choke tubes are interchangeable. Note the barrel porting, to reduce recoil and muzzle jump. Such systems invariably increase muzzle blast and can be annoying to nearby shooters, as well as damaging to hearing.

1866, the concept originated well before that time, informally and in various countries. Constriction did not work well with muzzleloaders, but, with the advent of breechloading, it became feasible. Gun makers began applying it in the 1870s. In England, the greatest proponent was W.W. Greener, and, in America, Fred Kimble.

At first, there was only one degree of constriction, "Choke," or what we would now term "Full." Later, gun makers began to vary the amount of constriction, applying different labels to different degrees, defined by the percentage of pellets in the pattern.

A barrel with no constriction at all is referred to as "straight cylinder," or simply "Cylinder" (Cyl.). A fully choked barrel is Full (F). In between, there are degrees of choke. In the United Kingdom, these are denominated in fractions (¼, ½, ¾) and, in America, Improved Cylinder (IC), and Modified (Mod. or M). In recent years, there have been variations and subdivisions, including Skeet No. 1, Skeet No. 2, Light Modified, Improved Modified, and Extra Full. Although this seems hideously complicated and confusing, it can be simplified very easily, and all considerations of degrees of choke rendered irrelevant, by simply hitting what you shoot at.

Degrees of choke are defined by pattern percentages, measured by firing a shot at 40 yards, drawing a 30-inch circle around the greatest concentration of shot, and counting the pellet holes. Full choke requires a 70-percent pattern, Modi-

Perazzi now gives its choke tubes numbers, rather than designating them IC, Mod., or Full. Some find this a confusing approach to identification, but it is really quite a simplistic system, one that provides general pattern percentages, rather than the "guarantee" of a pattern percentage some shooters think they need for a choke to be what it says it is.

fied 60-percent, and Improved Cylinder 50-percent. So, for example, if an ounce of No. 7½ shot contains 345 pellets, then 241 need to go into the 30-inch circle for the choke to qualify as Full.

The exception to this system is the .410, whose patterns are measured at 25 yards using a 20-inch circle, according to the *Hodgdon Shotshell Data Manual*; other authorities say 30 yards.

Choke is the most overrated and least understood facet of the modern shotgun. Partly, this stems from terminology, especially the use of the word "improved," as in "Improved Cylinder" or "Improved Modified." The implication is clearly that a tighter choke is a better choke, and this is simply not true in the vast majority of cases.

Over the years, the use of different chokes has led to a number of conventions. For example, IC is associated with brush guns and is normally chambered in a shorter barrel. Full choke is associated with waterfowl and used in longer barrels. With side-by-side doubles, the conventional combinations are IC/M or M/F. In the former case, the barrels are likely to be 26 inches long, in the latter, 28 inches. For right-handed shooters and side-by-side guns, the right barrel is normally the more open choke, the left the tighter choke.

In the early years, there were only "Choke" and "no choke," but the latter was not so marked. Thus, a gun from 1890 might be marked on one barrel "Choke," with no indication on the other as to what

A graphic demonstration of the shape a shot charge assumes at different distances in various degrees of choke.

The shape of a shot pattern as seen from behind. It shows how the pattern deteriorates from its widest and most even distribution, as distance increases. A Modified constriction pattern is the most even and, so, the most useful over a wide range of distance. *Photos these two pages by Gil and Vicki Ash.*

the constriction is. That gun, in modern terminology, would be Full and Cylinder, since before choke was invented there was only the unrestricted cylinder for and, so, no need to mark it in any way.

Experimenters found early that too much constriction was far worse than none at all, since it resulted in patchy, erratic patterns.

Choke is measured in thousandths of an inch, the bore diameter at the muzzle compared to bore diameter nine inches from the muzzle. Full choke ranges from $^{40}/_{1,000}$ to $^{45}/_{1,000}$ of constriction, whereas IC is seven to $^{10}/_{1,000}$, and the various Modifieds running $^{15}/_{1,000}$ to $^{25}/_{1,000}$. These figures apply only to 12-gauge; in smaller gauges, fewer thousandths of an

Gil and Vicki Ash, shooting instructors from Houston, have done extensive work studying shot patterns and creating models that give an excellent visual demonstration of how shot patterns evolve at different distances from the various degrees of choke. From the look of it, Modified may be the best all-around choke at varying distances, while Improved Cylinder is the most useful overall.

inch are required to gain the same effect, since what counts is relative, not absolute, measurement. In a 28-gauge barrel, Full is $^{22}/_{1,000}$ (London Proof House standard).

Because bore diameter can vary considerably, simply measuring the diameter at the muzzle will not tell you what choke you have. For example, the nominal diameter for 12-gauge is .729-inch, but it can run as low as .720 or as high as .740. It's all relative. For this reason, the old wives' tale about fitting a dime into the muzzle of a gun to check choke tells you, as Jack O'Connor wryly put it, only two things: "You have a dime, and you have a gun." The pocket choke gauges are better, but not absolute.

If one were looking for a rule of thumb for the average shotgunner who wants to know what choke to use, it would be this: less choke is better than more choke, 90 percent of the time. In game shooting, Full

has extremely limited applications. The vast majority of game birds brought to bag are shot at ranges less than 40 yards, and most of those at less than 30. Tales abound of miraculous kills at 60, 70, and 80 yards, but most of those exist only in the telling, not in the doing. For every opportunity you get to shoot at a bird at those ranges (considerations of ethical sportsmanship aside), a Full choke gun will cost you many misses at closer ranges and, if you do happen to nail a bird squarely with a Full choke gun at 20 yards, there will be nothing left to eat.

The only applications of Full choke are for trap shooting (and, even then, only for the better shots), some of the more extreme sporting clays targets, box-pigeon shooting, and for pass-shooting at ducks and geese. Tales of needing a Full choke and heavy loads for wild pheasants flushing at 70 or 80 yards in the Dakotas, are hogwash,

The Cutts Compensator was an early form of exchangeable choke device, offered as a factory option on some guns or as an aftermarket addition for others. The Cutts worked well, but was cumbersome and added nothing to the gun's appearance. Also, it worked only on single-barrel guns.

pure and unadulterated, under almost any realistic condition you can name. Like ultra-high-powered rifle scopes and yarns about shooting game at a thousand yards, stories about long-range shotgunning originate mostly in the imagination.

The shotgun is a 15- to 45-yard proposition at best, for the vast majority of shotgunners and the vast majority of birds, and chokes should be chosen for their application to those ranges. Cylinder is a very useful choke (almost abandoned, until recent years), IC a close second, and Modified very probably the best all-around choke of all, as measured in terms of its effectiveness over a range of distances. Modified gives you a very good pattern from 20 yards to 40, whereas Full is good at 45. Improved Cylinder starts to fall off quickly after 30 yards.

This line of thought can lead us into a morass of qualifications, and anyone seriously interested in studying what degrees of choke actually produce at genuine tested ranges, is

referred to the work of Gil and Vicki Ash, of Houston. The Ashes are shooting instructors and experimenters of a high order, and their work on choke patterns is a revelation. Their most significant finding, after firing thousands of rounds at pattern sheets at distances from 10 yards to 50, is that regardless of choke—*regardless*!—there is a 12-inch diameter core pattern of shot that extends the entire distance. In other words, if your pattern is dead-on at 40 yards, it doesn't much matter whether you are using Full choke, Cylinder, or anything in between.

Because there are so many variables in wingshooting, few of us ever make such a perfect shot. Where choke then becomes helpful is in turning the near misses into hits. Gil and Vicki Ash created three-dimensional renderings of the evolving shape of shotgun patterns, fired from guns with different chokes, over different distances. Some of these three-dimensional renderings are shown in the accompanying photographs. A glance tells you that Modified may well be the most useful choke of all, followed closely by Improved Cylinder, with Full a distant last for most applications.

Using one of the "all or nothing" choked English doubles from a century ago gives the best object lesson. Your obedient correspondent is, and always will be, I fear, a terribly streaky shot, both good streaks and bad, dotting an average career. In November 2008, though, I struck a vein of purest gold, while hunting wild pheasants in South Dakota.

We hunted them in grass, in conservation reserve plots, along the edges of corn and cane fields and through patches of woods. I was armed with an E.M. Reilly boxlock, dating from around 1888, with 30-inch Damascus barrels choked, in modern parlance, Cylinder and Full. During four days of shooting, I put together a string in which I killed 13 pheasants with 15 shots. The limit is three cock-birds per day; the thirteenth bird was knocked down, but not found. Significantly, that was the second bird of my only double and the only one hit with the left (Full choke) barrel. The 12 dead birds in the bag were all killed with the right (Cylinder) barrel, using B&P 1-ounce loads of No. 7 shot.

One such experience is hardly proof, but I have hunted with the same people in South and North Dakota, sometimes two or three times in a season, every year since, and we have all noticed the same trend: Those in our party with light loads of small shot and open chokes consistently collect more pheasants, while those using tight chokes and heavy loads of large shot collect fewer. There are several factors involved here, obviously, but the degree of choke is undoubtedly an important one.

* * *

In the London fine-gun trade, a client could order a gun and specify the exact chokes required in each barrel, down to and including shot size and his favorite load from Eley or from the gun maker's own proprietary ammunition. The gun would be finely tuned by the finisher or barrel regulator at the shooting range, adjusted one pass of the file at a time, until the barrels shot precisely where they were supposed to and delivered beautiful, even patterns of the exact percentage demanded. Also, because each gun was made to order and the client knew what constrictions had been specified, some London gun makers would not mark the choke on the barrels.

Holland & Holland follows that unmarked practice to this day with its bespoke guns, although not with guns made for stock sale. James Woodward & Sons, one of London's handful of very best makers, was renowned for returning barrels to their barrel maker if they missed the desired pattern by even one pellet on average, or if the pattern was in the least bit patchy or inconsistent.

In the heyday of box-pigeon shooting, clients could also specify what percentage of their pattern they wanted above and below a horizontal line on the pattern board at 40 yards. This practice is still followed today by makers of over/under competition guns. Adjustable ribs, available on the best competition guns, allow shooters to make their own such alterations.

In the white-heat competitive world of London gun making and live-pigeon shooting, with thousands of pounds and invaluable corporate reputations on the line, gun makers were not content to simply adopt a choke design and follow it. Variations appeared, some better, some not. One common variation was the "tulip" choke or, as it was called in America, the "jug" choke. In this design, the barrel walls are reamed out to a greater diameter four or five inches from the muzzle, then narrowed back down at the muzzle. This results in a muzzle diameter not much narrower than the bore itself. While this could appear to be little more than an

Improved Cylinder choke, it might actually deliver much tighter patterns. Indeed, tulip chokes were touted as delivering a superior pattern over a longer distance.

Measuring such a choke requires a bore gauge, not just a pocket choke gauge. Even then, the results can be very misleading if you do not measure the bore every inch or so from the muzzle to about six inches down. I have an H.J. Hussey pigeon gun from 1904 that has such chokes; by modern standards, they would be judged to be both Light Modified, but the left barrel delivers a noticeably tighter pattern than the right. The gun can be used effectively for everything from skeet to handicap trap.

Some American gun makers have applied the principle of the tulip choke to the entire barrel, boring them out to .740 or more the entire length, before tightening them at the muzzle. This is reputed to reduce recoil, as well as improve patterns.

* * *

For years, the great knock against single-barrel guns was that they did not offer a choice of chokes. Gun makers tried to get around this by offering replacement barrels in different lengths and chokes, which works only in a very general way. It certainly does not offer an *instant* choice. So inventors began working on adjustable chokes, devices that could be attached to the muzzle and tightened or opened up. The Poly-Choke, popular in the 1960s, was an adjustable device, while the Cutts Compensator was a set of detachable chokes.

The Cutts and the Poly-Choke were offered as factory options by some gun makers. Their great drawback was that they added weight to the end of the barrel and they looked, frankly, ugly as sin. The bulbous growth on the end of the barrel distracted the eye. Still, the inventors were on to something. The answer, obvious today but a break-

through back then, was the detachable screw-in choke that left the muzzle looking clean and uncluttered. Not only that, these devices could be used in double guns, especially the increasingly popular over/under.

With the arrival of interchangeable choke tubes, the over/under achieved a level of versatility no other gun can even dream of. Today, interchangeable choke tubes have become all-pervasive, even on low-priced shotguns. On the surface, this would seem to be a benefit for both shooters and manufacturers, since a shooter can now decide exactly what choke he wants in which barrel and even make changes between stands on a sporting clays range. As for the manufacturers, every barrel can now be exactly alike in terms of choke, which is a significant cost savings on the production line. At the same time, they can offer choke tubes in a mind-boggling array of constrictions with exotic names, creating a substantial secondary market.

There are, however, two things to keep in mind. First, regardless how a choke tube is designated (Cyl., IC, M, IM, etc.), there is no guarantee it will deliver the promised pattern in your particular gun. As well, different tubes in your gun may center the pattern in a different place, and even these results will vary, sometimes significantly, from one shot load to another. Only testing on a pattern sheet can tell you, but few shooters ever do this.

Some shooters fixate on percentages and loudly condemn a tube marked Full that delivers only a 68-percent pattern with a particular load, instead of the "required" 70-percent. To forestall this, some manufacturers (notably Perazzi) no longer mark their choke tubes with the traditional designations, instead simply giving them a number (No. 1, No. 2, No. 3, and so on, up to No. 10), and listing approximate pattern percentages that can be expected. This is definitely a step forward, if one must use choke tubes, in that it recognizes there are

Barrels in production at CSMC, in Connecticut. Longer barrels are once again popular in the smaller gauges.

no absolutes, especially with the enormous variety of shotshells available today.

The second consideration to keep in mind is that the very choice of choke tubes that seems like such a benefit can, in fact, be a trap. Stand with some shooters waiting their turn at a sporting clays stand and listen to the conversation. "What choke do you think? What was he using? Would this be better?" The buzz of battery-operated choke wrenches pervades the air. The shooter who then misses his first bird, for whatever reason, starts to second-guess his choice of choke. His confidence is undermined, and that is deadly to good shooting. Even when hunting game birds, shooters will change chokes after a pass through some grass because two birds flushed far out, then, with the Full tube in place, encounter a bird that goes up from under their feet.

Having many different chokes available tempts us to overanalyze situations. Having encountered birds a certain way in a field one day, the shooter sets up his gun to meet that situation next time he's there. The chances of any of it ever recurring exactly the same way, of course, are nil. Compare this with the old days, when a shooter had one gun, say, a Winchester pump, with a 28-inch barrel choked Modified. Long experience told him what that gun would and would not do. He knew the shots that were too long, and he also knew when to let a flushing bird get a little farther out, so that he could utilize the pattern effectively and not mangle tomorrow's dinner. This required little thought, long experience having made it unconscious habit. Because there was no choice, the gunner made do with what he had, concentrating on simply making the shot. There was no self-doubt, no second-guessing.

Confidence and instinctive reaction are no small things, when it comes to shotgunning. Faith in one's gun, one's swing, and one's instinct are essential elements of consistent good shooting.

BEADS AND RIBS

The rib is the narrow piece of steel that runs between the barrels of a side-by-side double, along the top barrel of an over/under, or atop any single barrel.

In a side-by-side, the original purpose was to fasten the barrels together and prevent moisture and grime from getting in between them. Gradually, gun makers discovered that the rib could be an aid to sighting and different styles could be selling points for their guns. On an over/under or single-barrel gun, this is the rib's only real function.

The bead is a small globe of ivory, brass, or silver set into the rib or directly into the barrel at the muzzle. It is not a sighting device in the normal sense of the word, since a good shooter could do without it quite easily. However, a bead gives the barrel a finished look. Everyone uses them.

Today, both ribs and beads have become as elaborate as the designers' fevered imaginations can make them, and the gaudier ones are used as sighting devices by trap and sporting clays shooters. For the

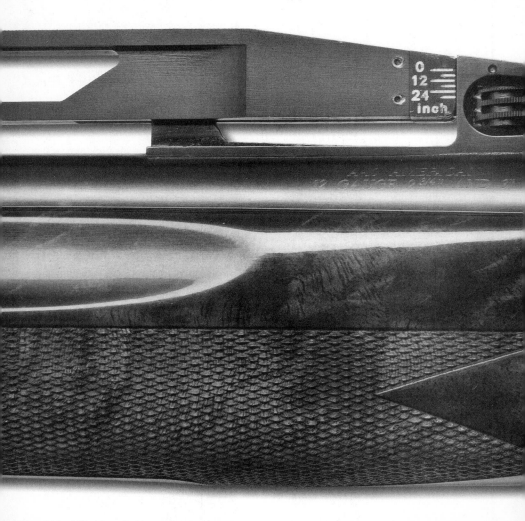

game shot, however, the simpler and less obtrusive the better, for both rib and bead.

Initially, the rib on a side-by-side followed the curve of the barrels, and the top surface of the rib was concave and polished blue. If this caught the light at all, it did so as a narrow "V," leading the eyes naturally to the muzzle and beyond, to where the eyes then picked up the target. Pigeon shooters, the earliest competitive gunners, found that a wide rib, cross-hatched to prevent reflection, served them better.

Gradually, certain conventions grew to be ribs appropriate for different purposes. The Churchill rib, for example, is quite high, tapering inwards toward the top and also from breech to muzzle. According to Robert Churchill, its originator, such a rib gave his 25-inch barreled guns the optical illusion of extra length.

A client ordering a gun from one of the Spanish custom gun makers might have the option of a concave, flat, knurled, ventilated, or Churchill rib, applied to any gun or barrel length he might choose. The ventilated rib

Ribs on ultra-modern competition guns, like this Galazan A-10 trap gun, are elaborate and fully adjustable. Photo by John Giammatteo.

The business end of a Galazan A-10 trap gun, complete with a high adjustable rib, interchangeable choke tubes, and a bright red bead.
Photo by John Giammatteo.

is now seen as the mark of a higher quality gun, at least on those made in the U.S. The Winchester Model 21, in its higher grades, had a ventilated rib rather than a solid one. On those, the utilitarian rib that connects the barrels had a ventilated rib mounted atop it.

As is their wont, trap shooters have often carried ribs to ridiculous extremes. Some of today's high ribs look like step ladders and are adjustable to get exactly the right angle between eyes and barrel, so as to put the pattern where the shooter wants it. In between the original swamped rib of a century ago, which demurely followed the barrels' contour, and today's modern high competition rib lies every variation imaginable.

Similarly, beads have become outlandish. First came the additional mid-rib bead, located halfway down the barrel. Viewed by the shooter, the two beads, ideally, form a figure-eight, showing the gun is correctly aligned and not canted. This can be helpful for anyone who pre-mounts their gun before shooting, as trap shooters do. After this, came ever more elaborate front beads. Today, it is possible to buy beads that consist of a four-inch piece of orange or green fiber optic plastic, glowing like a demented firefly. These beads are as interchangeable as choke tubes. For some competitors they work, for others they do not. Most good competition shooters want nothing distracting on the muzzle, which, alas, most of these elaborate beads are.

Like all gadgets that are billed as a panacea for your shooting ills, elaborate beads and exaggerated ribs should be viewed with a jaundiced eye, experimented with judiciously, and not be expected to perform miracles. A poor shooter is a poor shooter, regardless what bead and rib his gun is wearing—and he is often a poorer shooter *because* of the bead and rib.

CHAPTER 5

THE SHOTSHELL

This Gibbs & Pitt's 12-bore (here and on the following page), made in the 1870s and with a 2½-inch chamber, survived 40 years of 2¾-inch magnum duck loads with no apparent ill effects. This is more a tribute to the strength of the action than to the advisability of shooting cartridges longer than for which the chamber allows.

Shotguns are made today in six basic gauges: 10, 12, 16, 20, and 28, and .410-bore. As with most things to do with shotguns, the conventions and terminology are rooted in the practices of more than a century ago. Essentially, the guns and shotshells we use today were developed and perfected by 1900, and those now in use are merely refinements of very old designs.

SORTING OUT THE GAUGES

We should begin with the term "gauge" itself or, as it is called in Europe, "bore."

Unlike rifles and handguns, whose calibers are the measurement of actual bore diameter, shotguns use terminology descended from early cannons. In the Napoleonic era, cannons were sized by the weight of the round ball they threw. Hence, the famous British 12-pounder hurled a 12-pound projectile.

Handheld firearms were identified by the number of lead balls of equal size, making up a pound, that would fit the bore. Using the earlier terminology, if a pound of lead were divided into 12 equal parts, and each twelfth was formed into a perfect sphere, it would be .729-inch in diameter and the gun

Federal is the only American company still producing paper shotshells, and only in its 12-gauge Gold Medal competition loads. Trap and skeet shooters swear by them.

called a "one-twelfth-of-a-pounder." This was awkward, so it was shortened to 12-bore or, in America, 12-gauge. In a 16-gauge, there would be 16 balls to the pound, in a 20-gauge, 20, and so on. The exception is the .410, which is an actual caliber. In terms of gauge, a .410 is about 68-gauge. So, we have the somewhat confusing situation in which the smaller the number, the larger the gun.

In the muzzleloading era, bore diameter could be anything the maker or shooter wanted, since powder and shot were poured down the bore from the muzzle end; the only part of the ammunition that was sized was the wad, and those were usually cut by the shooter. With the advent of breechloading and self-contained ammunition, gauges were standardized. In the blackpowder era, there were 2-, 3-, 4-, 6-, 8-, 10-, 12-, 13-, 14-, 16-, 20-, 24-, 28-, and 32-gauge. As blackpowder gave way to smokeless, the number of gauges was reduced, with only the most efficient and popular retained.

* * *

A modern shotshell's internal components are essentially the same as in muzzle-loading days. There was gunpowder, an over-powder wad, a charge of shot pellets, and a wad to hold the pellets in place.

In today's standard plastic shotshell, the over-powder wad is a plastic shot cup that not only provides a gas seal, but cradles the shot as it goes up the barrel; in place of the over-shot wad there is the mouth of the shell, which is folded into a pie crimp. Modern shot cups tend to tighten patterns, which is not always desirable.

Each component serves a vital purpose, some more than just one. For example, the primary purpose of the over-powder wad in a blackpowder shotgun is to keep the powder packed firmly, the shot charge separate from the powder, and to act as a gas-sealing piston. It also cushions the shot from the initial pressure spike, thus preventing deformation of the pellets.

The shotshell evolved gradually, beginning around 1850, with the first breechloading guns. The idea of loading a gun from the rear had been a goal of gun makers for years. Having achieved a method of opening guns and fastening them closed, they then needed a convenient way to pack the powder and shot into the breech. The theory of the self-contained cartridge (from the French *cartouche*), had been around for some years, with the military issuing rolled paper packets that contained powder and ball, the paper serving as the wad.

From this basic idea emerged the pinfire cartridges used by the first breechloading guns. Instead of the hammer striking a cap perched on a nipple and sending a streak of flame into the gun to ignite the powder, a pinfire cartridge had a pin that extended into a cartridge. The hammer struck the pin, the pin struck an internal cap, and the cap detonated the powder. The cartridge case, complete with pin, was then pulled out of the chamber and replaced with a new one.

The pinfire cartridge case was made of rolled paper and brass. For the next 50 years, ammunition makers experimented with rolled- and drawn-brass cases, paper, combinations of them, and even aluminum cups wrapped in paper. The goal was to create a shotshell that was efficient, consistent, and powerful, as well as resistant to moisture. Eventually, the paper case—rolled, multi-layered, waxed paper, set in a brass cup—emerged as the most cost-effective pattern, remaining so until the 1960s, when plastic cases made their appearance.

A significant factor in shotshell design and manufacturing was the powder. Blackpowder was the early propellant. It occupies considerably more space than the various smokeless and semi-smokeless powders that began to replace it, in the 1880s. Since the sizes of bores and cases were already established—and since an ounce of lead shot occupied the same space regardless the propellant and, so, could not be altered—manufacturers had to find some way to take up the excess space in the case. They did this by filling up the space between the powder and shot with more wads, usually made of cushioning wool felt. After 1960, such wads were replaced by plastic shot cups of varying design, some simple, some bizarre, some patented and exclusive. Shotshell manufacturers guard their shot cup designs jealously and make claims for them ranging from improved patterns to reduced recoil.

The one great truth that emerged from all the research and development of shotshells, from 1850 to 1960, is that the laws of physics governing the behavior of a round lead pellet flying through the air dictate shotshell performance, and these laws of physics do not change. The corollary is that optimal shotshell performance is achieved by avoiding extremes, whether of shot size, charge weight, powder charge, or velocity. Moderation delivers the best results.

* * *

Federal Gold Medal Paper shotshells go well with a vintage trap gun, like this 1921 Ithaca.

Of all the gauges, in theory, the 16 should be the most useful and popular, for both ballistic and practical reasons. Each 16-gauge lead ball is exactly one ounce, and an ounce of birdshot, in a 16-gauge, forms a shot column about as tall as it is wide. Again, in theory, such a shot column should deliver the best pattern.

Using the "rule of 96," which states that, for tolerable recoil and for the well-being of the gun itself, a gun should weigh 96 times the shot charge, a 16-gauge gun would weigh exactly six pounds—the Utopian game gun weight.

While the 16-gauge has always been very popular in continental Europe, the 12-bore became dominant in England and the United States. Today, in the U.S., the 16-gauge is the least popular of the three common larger gauges. The 12 still dominates, but the 20 is closing fast and the 16 is a distant third. The 16's also-ran status is usually blamed on the inventors of skeet, who decreed that the game would be officially played with only four gauges—12, 20, 28, and .410. Why the 16 was left out, who knows? It was very popular at the time and widely regarded as the "gentleman's gun," to differentiate it from the market gunners' 12- and 10-gauge shotguns. Whatever the reason for its omission, as skeet spread like wildfire, it resulted in a general neglect of both 16-gauge guns and ammunition, a situation that continues to this day.

* * *

Another factor to be considered when choosing a gauge is the length of the cartridge. Three of the gauges (12, 20, and .410) have a three-inch "magnum" version, which holds more powder and shot than standard lengths and delivers more lead downrange at higher velocities. We will go into greater detail about the cartridge lengths available in each gauge, as we look

at them in turn. There is, however, a general observation that can be made about all of them, and that is that a shotgun's effectiveness is determined by the quality of the patterns it throws, not by the number or size of the pellets, nor by their velocity.

Traditionally, the ideal pattern is described as resembling an expanding beach ball, as high and wide as it is deep, with pellets evenly distributed within this sphere. The shot charge begins to expand about 10 yards from the muzzle of the gun and continues to change shape until, 200 to 300 yards distant, the last pellet drops to earth. Because the pattern is dynamic and constantly changing and cannot be seen while it is in the air, pattern definition is a source of endless fascination and endless argument.

As we saw in the discussion of chokes, the degree of choke plays an important role in determining the shape of a pattern, but pattern quality also depends on a number of other factors.

The 16-gauge is, again, theoretically ideal, because its ounce of shot forms a shot column of the right dimensions to translate into the perfect pattern. Excessively long shot columns create problems that inevitably affect pattern quality. This is the reason that 1¼ ounces of shot in a 10-bore is better than in a 12, and the 12-bore delivers better patterns with 1¼ ounces than the same amount of shot in a 20-bore. Similarly, packing a full ounce of shot into a 28-bore does not give you the equivalent of a 16. This is not to say that longer cartridges and heavier loads do not have their uses, only that, in shotgunning, there is no free lunch. What you get over here you will have to pay for over there. Long shot columns result in strung-out patterns, like the tail of a comet, with the badly trailing pellets performing no useful function beyond the odd fluke kill or broken clay. The occurrence of such flukes does not begin to make up for the loss of overall pattern effectiveness.

A 16-gauge pump gun is a thing of ergonomic beauty. This one is a Winchester Model 12, from the 1930s.

Twelve-gauge shotshells come in so many sizes, shapes, and configurations, they are a source of both endless fascination (for collectors) and endless frustration (for historians). These are American shotshells, from the 1920s to the 1970s, both paper and plastic.

The five major shotshell sizes today, from left: 12, 16, 20, 28, and .410.

The names Nobel and Eley are iconic in England, Nobel being one of the original manufacturers of smokeless powder and Eley Brothers a long-time manufacturer of shotshells. This display shows just a fraction of their products, but the wads (on which are printed the shotshell's vital statistics) give an idea of the range.

To visualize why shot stringing occurs, imagine a large crowd of people jostling and shoving to get through a narrow theater door, pursued by smoke and flames. Inevitably, many end up crushed and trampled on the floor. Much the same thing happens when a long shot charge is pushed by expanding powder gases. The pellets closest to the pressure are crushed against the pellets ahead, becoming deformed either a little or a lot. Being no longer perfectly round, when they leave the muzzle, they lose velocity

A sampling of the sizes in which 12-gauge ammunition has been made over the past 125 years, from left: 2-inch, 2½-inch, 2¾-inch, 3-inch, and 3½-inch. Each has its uses, but the 2½ and 2¾ are the most common and, overall, the most useful.

more quickly and tend to veer off to the side. Either way, they accomplish nothing for the shooter.

Tests have repeatedly shown that the best pattern quality is achieved with velocities from 1,050 to 1,200 fps at the muzzle. Anything less and the shot won't spread properly, which is why the early low recoil, low noise loads from the mid-1990s delivered a pattern the size of a grapefruit. If velocities go too high, on the other hand, they tend to "blow" patterns, giving the shot charge a violent shove as it leaves the muzzle and either scattering or blowing large holes in the pattern.

These general principles of shotshell performance have been proven repeatedly since the 1880s, but shotshell manufacturers still go to great lengths in attempting to circumvent them. They have tried buffering shot with other materials and using different shapes and styles of plastic shotcups. They have tried, in so-called non-toxic loads, different metals and compounds for shot. With some of these, notably the irregularly shaped Hevi-Shot, stringing and patchy patterns became a fact of life. The manufacturer tried turning a vice into a virtue by insisting that a long, strung-out pattern

allowed you to shoot badly and still hit a bird with the tail of the string. This is grasping at straws on a grand scale—then again, shotshell manufacturers have a genius for selling us things we don't need.

An interesting tidbit is the fact that today, with plastic shot cups, the diameter of the 12-gauge shot load is about what the 16 was in the days of muzzleloaders. This means that the theoretical ideal, with modern shotshells, is a one-ounce 12-gauge load, not a one-ounce 16.

The standard method of patterning a shotgun is to erect a sheet of paper at 40 yards, fire a shot at it, draw a 30-inch circle around the main concentration of pellets, and count the holes. The number of holes inside the circle, as a percentage of the entire shot charge, defines the choke. What a patterning sheet fails to tell you is the front-to-back shape of the pattern itself, nor does it tell you when each pellet struck the sheet. What looks like a nice, even pattern with no gaps could be the result of a pattern that was strung out 15 or 20 feet in the air, with many of the pellets performing no useful function. But, on paper, it looks pretty good.

This is a load of Federal 000 buckshot, consisting of eight .33-inch diameter pellets. The buffering material helps cushion the shot against deformation upon firing.

12-GAUGE

The 12-gauge is the most popular and versatile of all the shotgun gauges in use today. It has been the standard for all wing-shooting in England for 150 years, and in America for a century. The 12 is the only gauge used for trap shooting and big money box-pigeon matches, and it dominates sporting clays competition. In hunting, the 12 is the usual waterfowl and turkey load; in areas where deer hunting is allowed only with shotguns, most hunters use a 12.

Twelve-gauge guns have been made in every imaginable configuration, including hunting, competition, and tactical guns, with chambers ranging in length from 2 inches to 3½ inches. The 2-inch 12-gauge originated in England, in the late 1800s, and was intended for very light guns. Chambers of 2⁵⁄₈ inches were common in England until the early 1900s, when the length was standardized at 2½ inches for game guns; English live-pigeon guns were often chambered for more powerful 2¾-inch cartridges, and waterfowl guns for 3-inch rounds. In America, length was standardized at 2¾-

inch, with 3-inch shotshells coming around 1930, and the huge 3½-inch in 1987.

In America, today, the usual 12-gauge cartridge has a 2¾-inch hull. This is the length from the rim to the lip of the case *when the case has been fired*. A loaded 2¾-inch shotshell with its lip folded over and crimped is only about 2¼ inches. Length is important because, while you can safely fire a shorter cartridge in a longer chamber, you should avoid doing the reverse.

A chamber is bored the length of its shotshell when that shotshell is fully opened. On firing, the case opens to its full length and should then completely seal the chamber. This being the case, since a 2¾-inch cartridge measures only 2¼ inches when loaded, you can easily slip one into a 2½-inch chamber. The problem is that it will not be able to open fully, which means the shot and plastic shot cup must be forced through a smaller opening. This raises pressures and potentially plays all sorts of havoc.

There are conflicting opinions as to just how damaging or dangerous this is. Some

The classic Brenneke slug, loaded in Europe, was for many years the standard for 12-gauge slug loads for big-game hunting.

One of many experimental loads, as shotshell manufacturers try to make steel as effective as lead. In this case, we have the "squound," a pellet developed by Jay Menefee at Polywad. Each pellet is like a tiny Foster shotgun slug.

authorities would have you believe you are taking your life in your hands, or at least endangering your shotgun. One ammunition company, however, is reported to have run a series of tests and found no increase in pressures from the practice. This author is personally familiar with one instance in which a Gibbs & Pitt's-patent English game gun from the 1870s, with a 2⅝-inch chamber was subjected to a steady diet of

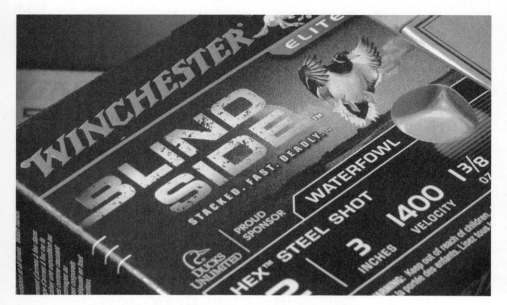

Winchester waterfowl load, with steel "rounded cube" pellets, designed to inflict maximum damage.

A few of Federal's specialty hunting loads for waterfowl and pheasants, where non-toxic (non-lead) shot is mandated. These shotshells pack some power.

Canadian 2¾-inch ammunition, including magnum duck loads, over the course of about 40 years. When the gun went in for a cosmetic restoration, the action was still tight as a drum. That could be merely a testimonial to the strength of that action. Having said that, it is impossible for the author to believe that subjecting any gun to such regular pressure spikes is not bad for it in the long term. At the very least, it cannot be good for it.

After 1945, as more and more English guns were brought into the United States, many of them had their chambers lengthened to 2¾ inches. For most, this is perfectly safe, though, on some very light guns, it could result in excessively thin barrel walls at the end of the chamber. Lengthening a chamber is an operation that should only be undertaken by a skilled gunsmith who understands the idiosyncrasies of double-gun barrels.

If you encounter such a gun and find that it does not pattern very well, or that the two barrels do not pattern together as they should, try shooting the original 2½-inch load. That, after all, was what it was regulated with. In one case, I found that an erratic gun became as sweet as honey, when I went back to the load for which it was originally chambered and regulated.

As with chambers, commercial 12-gauge ammunition is made in lengths from 2 inches to 3½ inches. Each has its purpose.

The 2-inch was an English development that received some attention in the late 1800s. W.W. Greener marketed it as "Greener's Dwarf," and guns so chambered were lighter than a standard 12—six pounds or less, as opposed to 6½ pounds. Charles Lancaster's version, the "Pygmy," caused considerable controversy with the editor of *Land and Water*, because of allegations of "shot balling." When shot "balls up," the pellets bond under pressure to become a single, highly hazardous projectile, endangering beaters (in driven shooting) and bystanders. Although the phenomenon was never proven, such short cartridges never enjoyed great popularity, probably because they were, to all intents, a 20-gauge charge in a 12-gauge shell. Such guns still appear for sale periodically, and you can order one from the English and Spanish custom gun makers.

You might wonder why anyone would go to that trouble and not simply buy a 20-gauge. The answer lies in the question of shot patterns, as discussed above. A ⅞-ounce load in a 12-gauge gives a shorter shot column than it does in a 20-gauge, with theoretical improvements in pattern. We should say, however, that too short a shot column is no better than one that is too long. Each gauge has its ideal range of charge weights, and ¾-ounce is about the smallest practical in a 12-gauge.

Up until 1914, many guns were made with chambers measuring 2⅝ inches; in America, this was later standardized at 2¾ inches, while the U.K. settled on 2½ inches. Then came development of the 3-inch magnum, followed, in 1987, by the mammoth 3½-inch. The 3-inch cartridge can take a charge load up to two ounces, while the 3½-inch, generally reserved for waterfowling or turkey loads, has a capacity of up to 2½ ounces.

With the advent of so-called "non-toxic" shot for waterfowl, in the 1980s, various lead substitutes were employed as shot material, including steel, bismuth, and different tungsten-based pellets. Since steel is less dense than lead, larger pellets are required to achieve the same killing power. At the same time, two ounces of steel occupy a larger space than two ounces of lead. The additional room in the longer case can be put to good use.

With many guns and a great deal of ammunition now being imported from Europe, chamber and cartridge lengths and charge weights are often given in metric measurement. For the record, a 2½-inch cartridge

Twenty lead balls weighing exactly one pound, hence the origin of the term "20-gauge."

is 65mm, 2¾-inch is 70mm, and 3-inch is 76mm.

20-GAUGE

The 20-gauge is the second-most popular gauge in use today, and for good reason. A 20-gauge gun, with its .612-inch bore diameter, is sleeker and less bulky than a 12 and can be built to weigh six pounds or even less. A pocketful of 20-gauge cartridges weighs noticeably less than the same number of 12s.

There are three cartridge lengths for the 20-gauge: The English standard 2½-inch, the American standard 2¾-inch, and the 3-inch magnum. Most mass-produced 20-gauge guns made today have 3-inch chambers.

While standard 20s are delightful to carry and pleasant to shoot, the 3-inch cartridge turns them into monsters. The magnum load is 1¼ ounces of shot, the same as a heavy 12-gauge game load. Most emphatically, however, this does *not* make the 20 the equal of the 12. A

1¼-ounce load in a 20 creates a long shot column, with all the negatives such a thing implies for patterns. Because you are forcing the same weight load through a smaller opening, higher pressures are required to achieve the same velocities. Combine all that with a 20-gauge gun weighing six pounds, and you have a nasty-kicking little beast that will induce a flinch in no time. The late Michael McIntosh was of the opinion that we would all have been better off if the 3-inch 20-gauge had never been thought of, and this author agrees wholeheartedly.

Having the 3-inch chamber but using only 2¾-inch loads does not give you something for nothing. If you order a 20-gauge gun with a magnum chamber from a European custom maker, it will be heavier and bulkier than a standard 20, because their proof laws demand it. So, you will be carrying around more gun than necessary, even if you plan never to shoot anything but 2¾-inch loads; you will have ordered the longer chamber only to enhance resale value. And

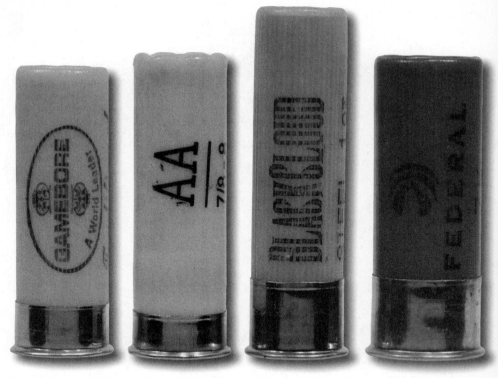

The 20-gauge is made in three different lengths. From left, 2½-inch, 2¾-inch, and 3-inch, with a 12-gauge 2¾-inch for comparison.

outside of waterfowling, the 2¾-inch 20 with either ⅞- or one ounce of shot will do anything desired, provided you are shooting within reasonable distances and put the shot in the right place.

In South America's high-volume dove shooting, the standard gun is a Benelli 20-gauge semi-auto, using 2¾-inch cartridges and either ¾- or ⅞-ounce loads. Those shooters routinely fire *two thousand shots in a day* and, if you think such light loads don't hurt, you try shooting in such numbers. *Everything* becomes a factor, from the weight of the gun to the effects on your shoulder, arms, and face. Semi-autos are favored, because they offer more shots before reloading, and also because they further tame even the mild recoil of a 20.

Contrary to popular belief, even the wildest of wild pheasants in the Dakotas will fall to a standard 20, if you place your shot correctly. One of the finest shots the author ever witnessed took place in North Dakota, on a day when the pheasants were riding a 60 mile per hour wind. Artist C.D. Clarke took a high pheasant at full speed, with a shot from his Arrieta 20, using B&P ¹⁵/₁₆-ounce ammunition. The wind carried the dead bird more than 60 yards in a long arc, with C.D.'s Brittany, Chess, coursing it all the way.

16-GAUGE

The 16 is the most logical of all the gauges. Its bore diameter is .662-inch, almost exactly two-thirds of an inch. A 16-gauge lead ball weighs exactly an ounce. An ounce of shot in a true 16-gauge bore creates a shot column of perfect dimensions for a good pattern.

The 16-gauge (center) compared to the 12- (left) and the 20-gauge.

In the United States, in the early years of the twentieth century, the 16 was known as the "gentleman's gauge." This differentiated it from the down-market 12, which was used by market gunners, farmers, and deer hunters. The romantic ideal of a 16 was a sleek double—a Parker, perhaps, or an Ansley Fox—intended for hunting upland birds like bobwhite quail and ruffed grouse.

The 16 comes by this patrician image honestly. Its antecedents go back centuries. In the era of blackpowder cartridge shotguns and rifles, 16-bores were made for hunting big game with solid ball, as well as for fowling. As we have already noted, on paper, the 16 is the perfect shotgun, the right size load creating the optimum shot column for delivering the perfect pattern from a gun weighing exactly six pounds. So what went wrong?

In Europe, nothing. There, the 16 is still very popular and was widely used in making combination guns like drillings. In England, the 16 was never as popular as the 12, but there were always a few around, and there still are. In fact, the last year or two has seen a fad for 16s; during a visit to Holland & Holland's Bruton Street shop, in late 2012, I saw a rack with a half-dozen 16-bore doubles just waiting for new homes.

In the United States, the 16's loss of popularity is generally blamed on the origi-

The 16-gauge is also made in different lengths. The 2½-inch (left) is archaic, but still beloved of some owners of old doubles, the author included. In the center is a European 67mm load, and right is the standard American 2¾-inch shell. The 2½-inch translates to 65mm, the 2¾-inch to 70mm. Some European companies make shotshells of 67mm, in different gauges, which can be used safely in either chamber length of the appropriate gauge.

nators of skeet. When the rules for skeet were drawn up, in 1926, it was decreed that the game would be officially shot with four gauges—12, 20, 28, and .410—and that left the 16 an orphan. You might think this would have had a minimal effect, but the course of events went roughly as follows.

With a widespread decline in game bird numbers and strict bag limits, shooters were left with trap and skeet, if they wanted to do much shooting. Trap, of course, is a 12-gauge game. Skeet spread rapidly, and soon manufacturers were making guns and ammunition tailored to its requirements.

Competition shooting eats up huge amounts of ammunition, and there was in-

tense rivalry among Federal, Winchester, and Remington, and several other companies no longer with us, to produce winning loads. Research money was poured into improving 12, 20, 28, and .410 ammunition, while the 16, which was no longer selling in anywhere near the volumes of the 12 or 20, was left to languish. Even the hulls were not as good; where a 12-gauge man could shoot Federal Gold Medal, Winchester AA, or Remington Premier STS and reload his own, 16-gauge shotshells used old technology and could not be reloaded nearly as well. When it comes to volume shooting, you need to be either independently wealthy or load your own, and successful reloading is dependent on components. Not only were good 16-gauge hulls hard to find, shooters were limited in their choices of plastic wads and shot cups. As well, lacking the volume-production savings of the 12 or 20, 16-gauge components were relatively expensive.

As for factory ammunition, manufacturers seemed determined to make the 16 the ballistic equivalent of the 12, presumably believing no one would shoot a 16 otherwise. Sixteen-gauge "heavy field" loads were hot and threw 1⅛ or 1¼ ounces of lead. In a standard-weight 16, they kicked badly, never patterned particularly well, and were expensive. Is it any wonder the 16 went into a steady, sad decline?

Today, there are essentially two cartridge lengths in 16-gauge, the English and European 2½-inch and the American 2¾-inch. Up until about 1914, there was also a 2⅝-inch on both sides of the Atlantic, and while you'll still see old guns with that chamber length, ammunition is no longer made. Fortunately, no one ever saddled the 16 with a 3-inch magnum version.

RST, the boutique ammunition company that supplies lovely, light loads in all different gauges and case lengths to keep old guns shooting and provide comfortable shooting even for new guns, makes 16-gauge ammunition to suit any gun ever made. More components are available today from reloading supply firms like Ballistic Products, and there is an increasing amount of reloading data for everything from low-pressure loads for vintage guns to hefty waterfowl loads using non-lead shot.

Ballistically, the 16 lies between the 20 and 12. It is at its best with shot charges of ⅞-ounce to 1⅛ ounces. A 16-gauge double weighing 6¼ pounds, with 30-inch barrels, is the kind of upland gun that grouse and woodcock hunters rhapsodize about (or bobwhite quail and dove hunters, for that matter). You can carry it all day and hardly

feel it, then shoot a hundred rounds and be ready for more. Unfortunately, in this era of non-lead shot for migratory birds, the standard 16 really doesn't have the case capacity to accommodate the bulkier steel-shot charges required, so it is best relegated to upland status.

The aura of the "gentleman's gauge" has crept into the limelight once again. America's classic doubles in 16-gauge, such as the Parker, Ithaca, Fox, and L.C. Smith, are in great demand on the used gun market and their prices are high. Still, if there is a bargain to be had in guns, it is in the 16-gauge pumps from years past—the Winchester Model 12, the Remington Model 31, and the Ithaca Model 37. In 16-gauge, these guns are a pleasure to carry and shoot, and they generally sell for considerably less than a 20 or 28 in comparable condition. And, if you can find a Belgian-made Browning in 16, whether it is a Superposed or an Auto-5, grab it. Those don't sell for peanuts by any means, but think of it as a lifetime investment in pleasant shooting.

Generally speaking, German and Austrian 16s from days past range from technically very fine to rather crude. What most have in common, alas, is that they are really not made for wingshooting as we know it. They are either combined with a rifle barrel or have excessive drop in a rifle-style stock.

I have strayed somewhat from discussion of the gauge itself into the guns that use it, but conversations about the 16 tend to do that. The reason? The 16 can be built into the ideal upland game gun, whether it in a double, pump, or semi-auto. The big ammunition makers are starting—tentatively, hesitantly, seemingly reluctantly—to offer some 16-gauge loads that are civilized in punch and recoil and still suitable for dove shooting or for an informal round of skeet. Magazine articles proclaiming the rebirth of the 16 are almost as numerous as those mourning its death. Here, in this book,

Wads from the transitional period between traditional fibre wads and modern plastic shot cups. These were made by the late Alcan Corporation, a major player in the shotshell component game in the 1960s.

The modern plastic shot cup, in this case, Federal's 12S0 (here and in the following pages). The cup protects the shot as it travels up the bore, and the compressible base cushions the shot charge against the initial pressure.

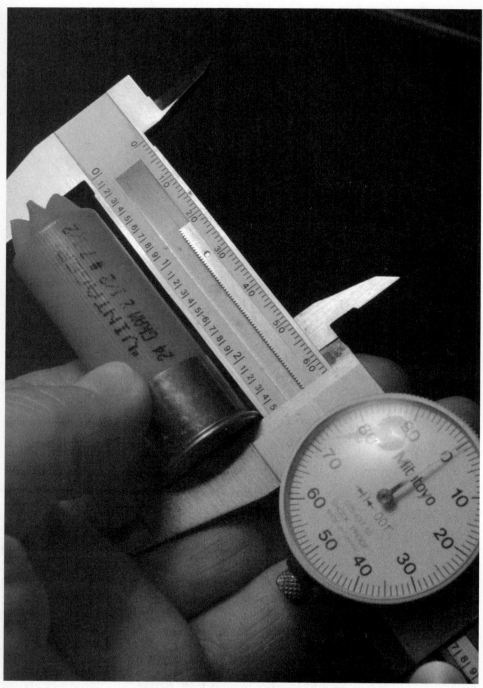

Case length is measured when the case is opened, not when it is loaded and crimped over. This is a 2½-inch case intended for English guns.

we are doing nothing except announcing improving signs of life in a lovely old gauge that deserves to be embraced by all.

28-GAUGE

Contrary to popular belief, the 28-gauge was not invented by Parker. Parker may well have been the first American gun company to chamber it, but it did not invent it. Like the 16, it is a very old bore size, one dating from the days of muzzleloaders.

When blackpowder cartridges replaced muzzleloaders, the 28-bore's career split, and it became the 28-gauge shotshell we know today, as well as the basis for the many .577-caliber rifle cartridges, including Holland & Holland's .577 Baker and the legendary .577 Nitro Express. England's military .577 Snider rifle was the 28-bore Enfield military musket converted to a breechloading brass cartridge. As late as the 1870s, .577 rifles sent to the London or Birmingham proof house for proofing were stamped "28" by the proof master, because that was the bore's gauge.

Just as the 16-gauge owes its shaky status to its exclusion from skeet, so, too, does the 28-gauge probably owe it current popularity, if not its very existence, to its inclusion on that list.

The 28-gauge has two cartridge lengths, the usual 2½-inch in England, and the 2¾-inch in America. Mercifully, there has never been a 3-inch 28-gauge. The very idea of attempting to convert the mild 28 into a 20-gauge equivalent with an ounce of shot, turning its five-pound guns into nasty little beasts, makes the blood run cold.

The 28 has a bore diameter of .550-inch, and standard loads range from ⅝-ounce to one ounce of shot. Because of the small bore, any shot size larger than No. 6 sits uneasily in the shot column; for game shooting, No. 7½ is probably best. Ballistically speaking, once you have a ¾-ounce of No.

7½s in the air, flying at 1,100 feet per second, it doesn't matter if they were launched by an overloaded .410 or an under-loaded 10-gauge, but one writer after another has rhapsodized about "killing power out of all proportion" in a 28-gauge.

This idea has given rise to several rather contradictory beliefs. One of these is the notion that it is somehow "more sporting" to use a 28, if you happen to be such an expert shot that you simply can't miss with a 12. The other is that the ¾-ounce of shot from a 28 is somehow more deadly than the same shot charge from a 12. Neither of these beliefs stands up to scrutiny.

Since the question of what is sporting and what is not arises most frequently in connection with the 28-gauge, this is a good place to deal with it. In wingshooting, the concept of a "sporting chance" is at odds with the goal of any ethical hunter, which is to kill game cleanly and without suffering. A 28-gauge gun with open chokes throws a pattern that covers the same area and is governed by the same percentages as a 20 or 12. But because the shot charge contains fewer pellets, you have a less dense pattern and, hence, a better chance that, even if you center your target, it will be struck by fewer pellets, thereby increasing the chance of wounding and losing the bird. If, however, you tighten the chokes on a 28 to increase the density, thereby reducing the overall size of the pattern, it does demand greater shooting skill to eliminate increasing the chance of wounding. But how many 28-gauge fans do this? Not many. Most 28s I have seen in the hands of hunters have had Improved Cylinder chokes.

The second belief illustrates the strange disconnect that can occur in the minds of people when promoting a cause. A few years ago, I encountered a 28-gauge proponent in North Dakota. His car stickers proclaimed his allegiances to the NRA, the Navy, and nuclear submarines and, in retirement, he'd become a gun writer for

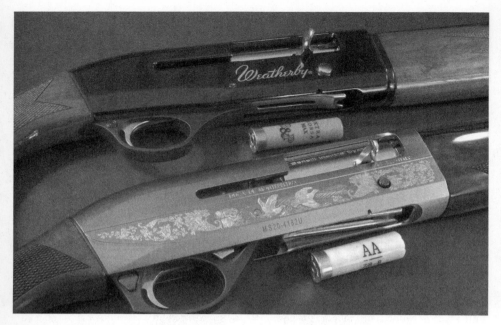

Comparing a scaled-down 28-gauge gun (top) with a 20. When a 28 is made on a scaled-down frame, as this Weatherby is, it is delicate and graceful.

the local weekly. He used a 28, he said, because a 12 was just too easy. "If you put the shot in the right place, three-quarters of an ounce will do the job," he said, even on North Dakota's wild pheasants.

No argument there. But then he went on to explain why, for wild pheasants with a 12-gauge, you need at least 1½ ounces of shot, preferably No. 4s, at 1,500 fps—a load that makes any gun under nine pounds a vicious mule. These two points of view are completely contradictory, unless you have a religious belief in the magical qualities of a bore that is .550-inch, instead of .729.

Many 28-gauge guns are too light and outfitted with barrels that are too short. As a result, they are very whippy. Hitting anything, for the average shooter, becomes extremely difficult. In recent years, the trend in 28-gauge barrels has been back toward 30 inches or even longer, with guns weighing right around six pounds. For a gun to shoot, this is about the ideal for most

people. Combine this with Modified chokes and ¾-ounce loads, and you have a gun that will challenge any good shooter, yet kill cleanly and break clays. Recoil will be almost nonexistent. If I were told I would have only that gun to shoot for the rest of my life, I would not feel particularly handicapped. In fact, it would be fun.

Because the 28 is a skeet gauge, there are excellent hulls and a generous variety of reloading components available. This is good because, if you want to shoot 28 in any quantity, the price of loaded ammunition will cause you to swoon. How something half as big as a 12-gauge can cost twice as much is an abiding mystery.

For a variety of reasons, 28-bore guns have never existed in great numbers. Those that do tend to be of higher grades and more expensive, whether old or new. Finding one the size and shape you want, at a price you can afford, is not easy. Many 28s made today are simply 28-gauge barrels stuck on

The three smallest gauges in regular use, from left: 20, 28, and .410. This shows how small the .410 really is.

a 20-gauge frame. This reduces costs, but does nothing for the shooter who is looking for a genuine 28-gauge. As well, the quest for an "all gauge" skeet gun that weighs exactly the same no matter what discipline you are shooting leads to 28s that are relatively heavy.

Every so often, a magazine article will appear touting the 28-gauge as some sort of "super bore" that can kill efficiently at ranges out of all proportion to its size. Generally, such articles are not written by professional shotgun writers, but by individuals who are riding their pet hobbyhorse. This is an important distinction to make, not to denigrate individuals, but to point out that professional shotgun writers, having been exposed to may different guns and loads, tend to be more restrained and moderate in their views on particular combinations.

Bob Brister, who was shotgun editor of *Field & Stream* for decades and wrote a very valuable book called *Shotgunning: The Art and the Science*, noted that the one-ounce load in the 28-gauge shared a characteristic with the classic live-pigeon load, which is 1¼ ounces of shot with 3¼ drams-equivalent of powder; that is, both seemed to be extraordinarily efficient. He even quoted one of Remington's shotshell ballisticians as being baffled as to why this should be, but insisting that it really was.

Given the time and effort Brister devoted to testing, especially patterning loads and trying to understand pattern shape, I am not about to argue with him. His explanation was that each seemed to achieve "balance." To Brister's duo, I would add the 12-gauge load of one ounce of shot and three drams-equivalent powder, which is a superb game load for almost anything that flies.

Balance is a very valuable concept in evaluating any shotshell load, and the subject has been espoused by every reputable shotgun writer from J.H. Walsh, in the 1880s, through Sir Gerald Burrard, in the 1930s, Gough Thomas, in the 1960s, and Brister, McIntosh, and others to the present day. Going to any extreme, whether it is shotshell length, charge weight, powder, velocity, or pellet size, tends to degrade patterns and performance and lessen efficiency and killing power. The 28-gauge is no exception. With the right ammunition and chokes, it's a great gauge, but it is not a magic wand.

.410-BORE

Without question, the .410 is the most controversial of all the bore sizes. Some experts believe it is not even a real shotgun round and has no place in any type of hunting. Others, including some very fine shots, insist it is "the expert's gun." They carry a .410 choked Full, their 3-inch shells are loaded with $^{11}/_{16}$-ounce of shot, and they shoot them with rifle-like precision.

For the average shooter, there is a slight perception problem with the .410. In terms of actual numerals, there is not much difference between 20, 28, and .410; if the .410 were numbered as a gauge, however, it would, in fact, be a 68. Maybe if we called it a 68-gauge, shooters would not give it more credit than it is due.

In truth, the .410-bore should be approached in a completely different way than with any of the other gauges. This has long been acknowledged by the convention of patterning the .410 at a different distance than the others. Choke designations for the .410 are defined by patterning at 25 yards, rather than 40. So, even with tight chokes, the .410 is a distinctly shorter range proposition than even a 28-gauge. In a way, the .410 is to shotguns what the .22 Long Rifle is to rifles and handguns: useful for certain purposes, a lot of fun to shoot, but a gun with limitations that need to be recognized.

Having said that, there is a great deal of interest in the .410. An entire book was devoted to the subject of .410s on both sides of the Atlantic, past and present, and there are gun collectors who buy nothing else. To the best of my knowledge, this is not the case with any other single gauge.

In America today, the most beloved .410 is the Winchester Model 42 pump gun— the Model 12 scaled down and chambered only in .410. It has achieved cult status, and prices are in an upward spiral. What sets serious .410 users apart from the 28-gauge crowd is that they are not judgemental, perhaps because they are so busy defending their own choice that they don't have time to deprecate others.

Aside from this small minority, the .410's most common application is as a "boy's" gun, and .410s are found in every configuration, from the cheapest of cheap doubles to Holland & Holland masterpieces. The average .410 is very light and has a barrel of 26 or, at the most, 28 inches. On a Model 42, such a short barrel is not a huge handicap, although longer would be better, but on a double it certainly is. The guns are so light and whippy, it is difficult to hit anything, even if you have an adequate shot charge.

Because of the difficulty of hitting anything, starting a child off with a .410, with any idea of turning him into a wingshot, is not doing him any favors. Repeated missing will discourage a kid faster than anything else. Yes, subjecting a child to excessive recoil is just as bad. The days in which you could give your son an Iver Johnson .410 and turn him loose with a pocketful of ammunition to roam the farm, shoot at whatever, and get the feel of it, are long gone for most of us and, with it, much use of a .410 as a training tool.

Of course, the .410 is one of the skeet gauges and, so, .410 barrels are available for any good skeet gun. They are longer, relatively heavy, and there is absolutely no recoil. They have a good swing, so if a child can handle the weight, they are useful for teaching. As with the 28-gauge, hunting with a .410 is a game of tight chokes, short ranges, and rifle-like precision of shot placement.

CHAPTER 6

LOADING YOUR OWN

Handloading shotshells is a tradition that goes back to the very beginning, to the era of pinfire shotguns and blackpowder. It has continued to this day, with improvements in loading equipment and components every bit as astonishing as they are in the guns themselves.

Handloaders—or, as they are called in England, "home loaders"—pursue this activity for a number of reasons. Probably the most common is expense. Serious trap and skeet shooters go through a large amount of ammunition in a week, and there is a substantial cost savings if you load your own. For people of average means, these savings can mean the difference between being a competitive shooter or not.

The second reason for handloading shotshells is to create a load you cannot get otherwise. This may be a very mild load in a particular gauge, the creation of ammunition that is no longer available, or it may be to load special shot, such as non-lead alternatives, where there is no commercial ammunition readily available. In this case, you might or might not save money, but you will get to shoot what you want.

A third reason is reliable supply. As I write this, in 2013, the U.S. is in the throes of an ammunition and component shortage of every kind, because of fear of political action against guns. Panicky shooters are buying up every type of ammunition, including shotshells. Those who routinely keep a generous supply of shot, powder,

and primers can continue shooting where others cannot.

The fourth reason for handloading, which is seldom mentioned and always underestimated when it is, is the simple pleasure of doing something gun-related, even on those days when a blizzard is blowing and you want to smell gun oil and handle some shotshells. Michael McIntosh once described his own ritual of preparing loads for a special gun he really liked for hunting ruffed grouse and woodcock, and how he would repair to his loading room with a glass of red wine and his pipe and lovingly prepare two-dozen cartridges by hand. Aside from the questionable practice of smoking around gunpowder and warnings about measuring powder while under the influence, I sympathize completely. Ritual is an important part of the joy of shooting.

* * *

A century ago, loading paper or brass shotshells was an activity that could be carried out at a kitchen table, around a campfire (with suitable precautions, of course), or in the back seat of a car. While commercial ammunition manufacturers even then used highly automated equipment to produce shotshells by the thousands, most handloaders produced a few dozen at a time, using four or five simple hand tools. These tools consisted of a capper and de-capper for priming; a sizer to return the base of the fired case to its

Federal's paper cartridge making facility in Anoka supports the one remaining paper mill that produces the coated paper suitable for such shotshells. It comes in big rolls that, about nine days later, becomes many shotshells.

original dimensions; a powder measure; a wad rammer (basically, a short piece of dowel with a knob); a shot measure; and a "turnover" tool for imparting the crimp. The components consisted of primers, powder, wads, and shot.

A handloader today can do much the same thing, using very similar tools. The Lee Loader for shotshells, the simplest of kitchen table setups, has always been inexpensive yet capable of producing ammunition out of all proportion to its cost. For that matter, if you are loading for an old gun or simply like to do things the traditional way, many tools made a century ago can be put back into service. There is a thriving community of collectors of old loading tools.

At the other end of the scale we have massive, automated, high-volume shotshell reloaders from companies like Ponsness-Warren, Hornady, or MEC (Mayville Engineering Company). These produce shells by the thousands, with the operator's job restricted to little more than feeding in empty hulls and keeping the hoppers full of primers, powder, shot, and wads. These machines can cost thousands of dollars, but, for a family of average means in which everyone shoots, every weekend, at trap, skeet, and sporting clays, it may be the only economical way to do it.

Although the initial investment in a shotshell loading machine ranges from a few bucks for a Lee Loader, to $3,000 for the state of the art, power-driven Ponsness-Warren, the cost of either can be recouped relatively quickly.

* * *

Most articles about handloading shotshells stress the ease of it all—how much money you can save, how simple it is, how convenient, how much fun. All of this is true, to a point. But, like most things to do

with shooting, handloading is an art and a skill, and learning to use even the most basic tools requires intelligence and application. Needless to say (at least, I hope it's needless), handling primers and gunpowder, either black- or smokeless, demands extreme care and close attention.

Although there are similarities to handloading rifle and handgun cartridges, there are also important differences. These differences will even surprise veteran loaders of metallic cartridges who turn to shotshells for the first time.

The most important difference is the critical nature of the finished product. With a rifle cartridge, within limits, you can seat the bullet as deeply as you desire, use different powders (whether they fill the case or not), and switch primers without affecting pressures unduly. Not so with shotshells. The components that go into the case must create a solid package, with the powder firmly packed and the crimp holding the shot solidly in place. This both makes the shotshell durable, holding together while rattling around in a shell bag, and provides resistance that allows pressure to build to the desired level when the round is fired.

Load data for shotshells gives specific information as to the brand of hull, brand of primer, type and amount of powder, weight of shot charge, and the specific wad or shot cup to be used. These loads are extensively tested combinations in which all the components fit together to give you a well-packed cartridge, at pressures within industry limits. There are many good shotshell loading manuals available, most notably from Hodgdon (the powder company) and Lyman (loading tools). These manuals include detailed information on primers, powders, hulls, wads, and shot cups, and they explain exact procedures for assembling them, step by step. Most important, they list vast numbers of

These are soon to be Federal paper hulls, at this stage rolled tubes cut to length and impregnated with wax, seasoning in a large bin under climate-controlled conditions.

The various stages and components that go into a paper hull. The long strip is rolled to become the base wad.

Ralph Gates, a shotgunner of the most depraved sort, in his loading room. He keeps 12 machines ready to load any of his dozen favorite loads, in a five different gauges, at any time.

loads, using all available components, with velocities and pressure information.

In a book such as this one, there is not room to even begin to duplicate the material found in these manuals, and anyone contemplating the game of handloading is advised to make a good manual their very first purchase. If nothing else, it will help guide you to the purchase of the loading equipment most suited to your needs. Our purpose is to give an overview of handloading, its benefits and procedures and, perhaps, spark an interest in a shooting-related activity that will not only save money, but will teach you a lot about shotshells, how they work, and how you can best put them to use. People who load a lot shoot a lot, and people who shoot a lot are generally better shots.

***

Two of the differences between metallic cartridge reloading and shotshells are the complexity of all but the most basic machines and their relative lack of versatility. A Lee Loader, for instance, is not very complex, but a progressive press that ejects a loaded round with each pull of the handle certainly is.

A progressive press has a rotating plate that moves the case from station to station, and there are many parts and adjustments. Each adjustment of each station must be perfect if the ammunition produced is to be acceptable quality. Getting a machine set up to produce just one load, in one gauge, with one set of components, is time consuming, and while it is possible for most machines to be converted with a different set of dies to load different gauges, it is finicky work. Most people who want to load a different gauge find it is easier, and almost

To the shotshell handloader, these hulls are pearls beyond price: Premium, once-fired Winchester Double-As.

as economical, to simply buy a second press in the different gauge. Compare that to metallic reloading, where you buy just one press and switch from one caliber to another, changing dies in a matter of minutes, or even having it set up to load three or four cartridges at the same time.

Shotshell loading presses are all multi-station. The difference between a progressive and non-progressive press is that the former has a circular moving plate with many stations, each of which holds a case in a different stage of loading. This plate rotates, moving each case forward one stage with every pull of the handle. The user of a non-progressive press moves each case by hand, shepherding hulls through the loading process one procedure at a time. The latter are easier to convert to a different gauge, but, by the same token, are so inexpensive that it is generally easier to buy a second press than to purchase the dies and go to the trouble of converting them, if you plan to load two or more gauges on a regular basis.

The final major difference between loading shotshells and metallic cartridges is the investment in components and the requirement for exact combinations of four or five different components, with little or no interchangeability. This is why you often find partial bags of wads for sale on bargain counters and why the sudden unavailability of a particular component can throw your whole loading operation into chaos. You are set up to

The MEC single-stage press in its many variations is the most popular shotshell reloading press in the world. Here, it is being used to produce 16-gauge loads using Federal field hulls. This press produces excellent ammunition, although not as quickly as more expensive progressive presses, but it's perfect for such a low-volume load.

load one brand of hull with a particular type of wad; then you switch to different factory ammunition as your source of hulls, that wad no longer works well, and you are left with a few hundred wads and no use for them. If you are of a finicky, perfectionist turn of mind, the logistics of reloading shotshells can drive you mad.

SHOTSHELL HULLS

If saving money is part of the goal, the hull is the most important single component. Which one (or ones) you choose to reload, how you collect them, and how you treat them not only dictates how much money you will save, but how well you will shoot with them.

Most modern shotshells are made of plastic, with metal bases. In years past, shotshells were also made of pure brass and brass and paper; both types are still available. In the United States, Federal Cartridge still loads its Gold Medal competition ammunition in paper hulls for shooters who prefer them, and Federal has the last facility in the U.S. for making such hulls. Demand from Federal supports the very last paper mill that still makes the specialized, coated paper, produced in huge rolls, from which the hulls are made. Paper hulls are still made in Europe, and in most gauges.

Brass hulls are still manufactured in Brazil, and they are available commercially in the U.S. Brass shotshells are almost inde-

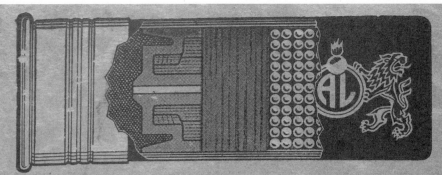

AIR-WEDGE® used over powder with FELTAN-BLUESTREAK® under the shot

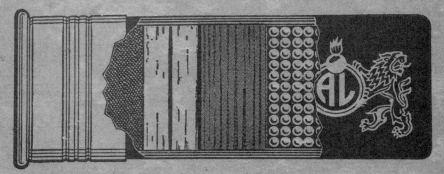

ALCAN nitro card used over powder with FELTAN-BLUESTREAK under the shot

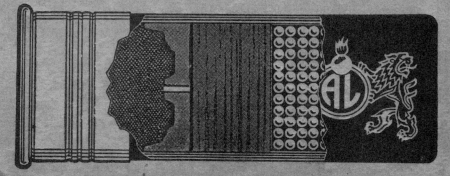

PGS plastic gas seal used over powder with FELTAN-BLUESTREAK under the shot

In the 1960s, the Alcan company of Alton, Illinois, was a titan of the reloading industry, producing everything from primers to wads to hulls. This old illustration shows the construction of a shotshell from the days when plastic wads were just coming into use.

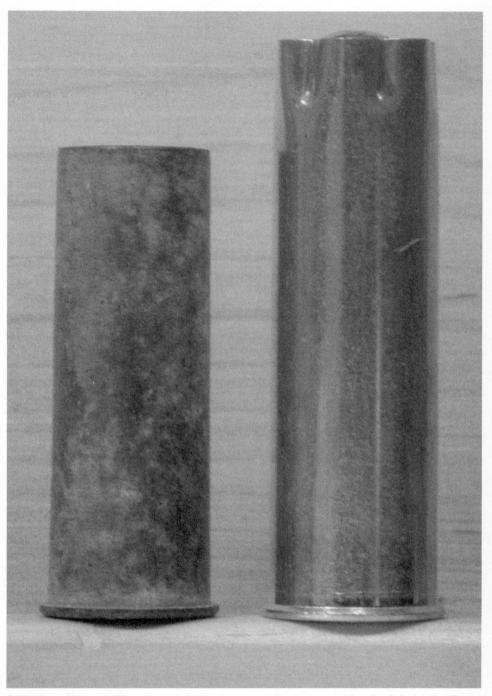

Original brass 20-gauge hull from the 1800s (left) beside a new-production brass hull from Brazil. Such hulls will last virtually forever if they are loaded carefully.

structible, when handled properly and loaded judiciously, and are very popular among shooters of blackpowder shotguns and those using obsolescent sizes like 4- or 8-bores.

The majority of shotshells loaded in the United States use Winchester AA hulls, and these are the standard by which all others are judged. Double-As are renowned for their ease of reloading, although Remington Premier, STS, and Nitro hulls are every bit as good, in my experience, and Federal Gold Medals very close behind. One advantage of these three is the vast amount of loading data available. As well, many of the progressive presses used by high-volume competition shooters come from the manufacturer already set up and tuned to load AAs, although they can be easily adjusted to the others. Using these presses for paper hulls can be an exercise in frustration, however, and brass cases are impossible on them.

As well as these hull types, there is a plethora of others on the market. The

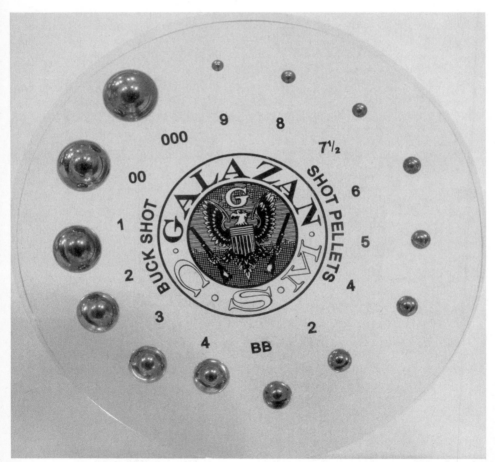

American lead shot in the common sizes now available, from the tiny No. 9 used for skeet to the mammoth 000 Buck used for deer and tactical loads.

hulls used for the ultra-low-priced "club" shotshells made by all the major ammunition companies, as well as those loaded specifically for big chain stores or to supply in bulk to shooting clubs for routine shooting, generally do not reload well. Nor are they intended to. Any shell can be reloaded if you proceed carefully, but not all are worth the effort.

The great virtue of the Winchester AA hull is that the plastic can be reworked many times without splitting or disintegrating, and its pie-crimps stay in place. Lower-quality hulls may split after only two or three uses, or the plastic mouths become "dead" and refuse to hold a crimp.

Plastic hulls consist of several separate components that are fastened permanently together. The very first plastic hulls, which appeared in the 1960s, had a brass base, a plastic tube, and a fiber base wad. Such hulls are called "Riefenhausers," named for their inventor, and they are still used in many applications. More modern cases, like the AAs, combine a one-piece wall and base wad with a metal base cup. This requires higher quality, more expensive plastic than that used for Riefenhauser shotshell, but this type of plastic is better for reloading. The point here is that one plastic hull is *not* necessarily like another. You should check hulls very carefully and ensure you have the hull specific to your loading data.

There are also what might be called "specialty" hulls. Baschieri & Pellagri (B&P), the Italian company, produces absolutely first-class ammunition with hulls that use the Gordon base wad. The Gordon system uses a compressible wad to help absorb recoil. These hulls can be reloaded, but caution is required. You need to be careful not to compress the base wad when loading the round, and you also need to be aware that, with each firing, the wad loses

some of its elasticity. Practically speaking, you can reload Gordon-system hulls two or three times only. Because of these difficulties, reloading data is almost nonexistent. If you find a plentiful supply of some obscure shell and can't find loading data for it, chances are there is some difficulty and you need to investigate further before attempting to use them.

Trap shooters (and some skeet shooters) are weird people. Some of them take an almost religious pleasure in squeezing as many loads as possible out of one hull. They can be seen at trap ranges, scrounging through discard bins, searching for AAs and other premium hulls that some other, less frugal shooter has discarded before every ounce of life has been squeezed from it. Their hulls are reloaded over and over, to the point where they are scorched black, the mouths are ragged, splits are appearing, and some are even held together with a piece of tape over the crimp. Their reloads sometimes fall apart in their shell bags, or the second round will give up the ghost under the recoil of the first in doubles shooting, and shot will dribble out the end of the barrel.

Embarrassing? Not to these folks. Some have even been seen raking through piles of spent wads, looking for shot cups that can be pressed into service a second time. Others have been known to sift the earth where the shot falls, separating the lead pellets for reuse. If these people were not stepping up to the line with a $10,000 Perazzi, all of this would be amusing. And, truth to tell, one can never have too many weird trap-shooter stories with which to regale the boys at the club. As someone who enjoys shooting trap, tries to shoot nice guns, and has agonized over discarding a hull because it seems to be developing cracks before its time, I feel I have a right to talk about this.

Federal shotshell primers.

The primer and how it fits into the base of the shotshell.

PRIMERS

Shotshell primers are generally *physically* interchangeable, but some primers are noted for being hotter than others. How a primer reacts with a particular powder is an important factor not only in consistency of burning, but in the violence of the reaction and the resulting pressures.

Loading data always specifies the primer used, by brand and number, and handloaders are advised to follow these instructions and not substitute. You will be is tempted to say, "But, if a particular primer is not available ..." and give instructions on how such substitutions might be safely carried out. Don't. There are too many variables and pitfalls, and the only safe course of action in the modern world of litigation is to say, "Go by the book, don't deviate."

In the interests of logistic simplification, it is wise to stick to loads that use many of the same components, with primers being the most obvious. It is also wise to buy your primers at least 10,000 at a time. A thousand shotshell primers don't go very far, when you burn 200 rounds in a day—not unusual for any trap shooter—and they don't go bad on the shelf if they are stored properly. Having a good supply on hand not only saves trips to the store, it is insurance against temporary shortages.

For some reason, aside from political considerations, primers seem to go through cycles of feast and famine. At least three shortages have occurred in the past 25 years

Although two primers may both bear the designation "209," each has its own characteristics and cannot be interchanged without affecting the ballistics of the load.

Hodgdon's three fine modern powders—Clays, International Clays, and Universal Clays—can be used to load virtually any shotshell for virtually any purpose. They are clean, economical, and effective.

RELOADING DATA CENT

For a complete listing of all our data go to www.hodgdon.com

GAUGE	SHOT WT.	HULL	PRIMER	WAD	CHARGE
12 ga., 2-3/4"	1-1/8 oz.	Win. AA	Win. 209	Win. WAA12	18.2 gr.
12 ga., 2-3/4"	1-1/8 oz.	Rem. STS	Rem. 209P	Rem. Fig. 8	19.2 gr.
12 ga., 2-3/4"	1-1/8 oz.	Fed. Gold Medal	Fed. 209A	Fed. 12S3	19.0 gr.

CALIBER	CHARGE	BULLET	CASE	PRIMER	C.O.L.
38 Special	2.5 gr.	148 gr. Hdy. LHBWC	Win.	Win. SP	1.160"
44 Special	4.6 gr.	165 gr. Cast LRNFP	Starline	Win. LP	1.365"
45 ACP	5.2 gr.	155 gr. Cast LSWC	Win.	Fed. 150	1.230"

MAXIMUM LOADS – DO NOT EXCEED – REDUCE PISTOL DATA BY 10% TO

NET WT 8 LBS. (3.63 KGS)

Shotshell loading data is very specific, as to combinations of hulls, primers, wads, powders, and shot payloads. One should not deviate or substitute components.

(1989, 1996, and 2001), aside from the panic buying of 2009 and 2013, in which primers were doled out by manufacturers, rationed by retailers, hoarded by shooters, and used as currency at gun clubs like cigarettes and stockings in post-war Europe.

GUNPOWDERS

Shotshells can be loaded with either black- or smokeless powder. The former is usually restricted to old guns or for use in competitions that specifically demand it, such as Cowboy Action Shooting.

Blackpowder is a mechanical compound (a simple mixture of charcoal, saltpeter, and sulphur), whereas smokeless powders are chemical compounds. Most smokeless powders have a nitroglycerin base.

Blackpowder generates lower pressures, which is easier on old guns. It also has a different burning pattern, which results in corresponding differences in shotshell performance. These were noted during the extensive testings that went on in the 1880s and '90s, when the first smokeless powders made their appearances. In those transitional years, some shooters used blackpowder for one purpose and smokeless for another, noting better long-range performance or reduced recoil. Today, powders are chosen for their suitability to a particular gauge more than their ballistic characteristics.

The drawbacks of blackpowder are that it is messy, requires thorough cleaning of guns immediately after use, and is tricky to reload. The billowing cloud of smoke every time you pull the trigger can be exciting or exasperating, depending on your attitude.

With old American guns, whether to use smokeless or blackpowder is largely a matter of personal preference and prudence. With European guns, where government proof houses certify guns for different uses, a gun with only a black-powder proof is not approved for use with smokeless powder. This does not necessarily mean it's unsafe with a smokeless powder, only that it has not been tested with smokeless proof loads and proven to be so. There are so many factors to consider here that, if you are in any doubt about an old gun, you should take it to a qualified gunsmith and have it thoroughly checked before you shoot *anything* in it.

Today, you can still buy factory-loaded blackpowder shotshells, but they are not cheap and can be difficult to find. As well, there are different shipping regulations for blackpowder than for smokeless, since the former is classed as an explosive. Anyone needing blackpowder shotshells who wants to do a lot of shooting is almost forced to handload. In many cases, there is no other way.

If you decide to load blackpowder, you will need paper or brass hulls. The detonating characteristics of blackpowder do not go well with plastic, either in hulls or shot cups. Then again, if you are returning to the world of blackpowder, you will probably want to use as many original components as possible, assembled with genuine Victorian implements. When you do so, and then use one of your own creations to bring down a bird on the wing in a cloud of smoke, it's a feeling quite unlike any other.

* * *

Modern smokeless powders are among the most advanced of all reloading components. Powders developed purely for competition shotshells combine consistent burning with low pressures and virtually no cleaning required afterwards.

Some older shotshell powders, like Red Dot and Herco, have some of the messy characteristics of blackpowder, leaving residue in the barrel, even if it doesn't actually promote corrosion. They are still loved by many shooters for their consistency and the quality of patterns they produce.

Once-fired hulls from Baschieri & Pellagri, the old (1885) Italian company that produces some of the most effective shotshells in the world. These hulls are fitted with Gordon-system compressible wads, to reduce felt recoil. While these can be reloaded, data is not readily available.

A selection of old-style fiber and cardboard wads, in 16-gauge. These are used to load blackpowder ammunition, for use in paper cases, or for low-pressure loads for older guns.

Shotshell powders are generally fast burning compared with rifle powders, with many doing double duty as both shotshell and pistol powders. Unique, the second-oldest powder still in use (it dates from 1900), from ATK (formerly Hercules), is the all-time champion, in this regard.

The larger the gauge, the faster burning the powder. In fact, the 28-gauge uses powders that are so slow burning they have little or no application in the 12-gauge. At the same time, the rule with rifles and pistols is that the heavier the bullet, the slower burning the powder, and the same is true of shotguns; you need to give the shot load time to get moving before the pressure peaks, otherwise it peaks too soon and too high.

With volume shotshell reloading, the size of the powder charge becomes a significant cost factor. Buying a powder that will deliver a suitable load with only two-thirds as much powder translates into significant savings over the course of months of shooting. Like primers, it is best to buy your powder in bulk. Shotshell powders are generally available in five- or eight-pound containers, and that is about the minimum that's practical, if you reload cases in any serious amount. Buying one pound at a time is only practical if you are experimenting with a particular load and don't want to make a big investment until you are sure it will work.

One caution: Sometimes you will find partial containers of powder for sale at gun clubs or on the bargain table at gun shops. Any opened container of powder is best avoided. You don't know what some fool may have done with it, like "salvaging" powders from unused cases, or emptying the hopper into the wrong container. Similarly, it is an excellent idea never to use anyone's handloads but your own, especially in a valuable gun—or if you value your body parts. You don't know what mistakes or misjudgments someone else might have made, and you don't want to pay the price for them.

Because it involves powder and powder measurement, this is a good place to explain the arcane term "dram equivalent." Blackpowder was measured by bulk, not weight, and particular loads were listed in number of drams. A dram of blackpowder weighs about 27 grains. The term "dram equivalent" does not refer to the amount of powder in a shotshell, but to its relative power or velocity. So, a box with "3 Dr. Eq." printed on it tells you that the load gives the power of whatever amount of shot is listed with that amount of blackpowder. Obviously, three drams of blackpowder will give a different velocity with one ounce of shot than with 1 1/8 ounces, which is why "dram equivalent" is really a power reading, not one of velocity. In recent years, more manufacturers have taken to providing velocities on their shotshell boxes, either alongside or instead of dram-equivalent ratings. We will delve into this more in the section on blackpowder shooting.

WADS AND SHOT CUPS

In original centerfire shotshells, overpowder wads were made of felt or cardboard, and the over-shot wad was a cardboard disc. Today, what we still call "wads" are really plastic shot cups, and they come in so many shapes and sizes it is impossible to describe even a few of them. What is important to remember is that they perform two vital functions and one that is optional. The vital functions are to hold the powder in place with a degree of compression, and also to provide a gas seal between the expanding gases of the burning powder and the shot charge as the shot travels up the bore. The optional function is the cupping of the shot, with the plastic petals of the wad providing a barrier between the shot and the walls of the bore. This protects the shot from deformation, if it is lead, or the bore from abrasion, if it is steel or tungsten. Also, if a buffer is used (a soft substance intended to cushion the shot), that buffer is also contained in the cup.

The thick felt and thin cardboard wads of a century ago performed exactly these same functions, with the exception of cupping the shot. Felt worked particularly well, because it could be of a small enough diameter to fit easily into the hull. As pressure was applied from behind, the wad compressed vertically and expanded horizontally, providing an excellent gas seal. The plastic wads of today may be more convenient, but they are not nearly so versatile. They do one thing well, but that's all they do, whereas felt wads can be used in different thicknesses, or even two or three at a time, to get the desired load characteristics.

Because their external dimensions must conform to recognized industry standards for chamber sizes, this means their internal dimensions vary. As a result, wads that work in one type of hull may or may not work in another. This is not a problem if you are working to a formula from a loading manual, but it can be a major concern if you are trying to assemble components for a custom load.

Felt and cardboard lend themselves only to one-at-a-time shotshell reloading, with either a Lee Loader or the tools of the nineteenth century, but, used judiciously, they deliver first-rate shotshells with excellent ballistic performance. An additional and increasingly important benefit of natural-fiber wads is that they are biodegradable and neither litter shooting areas nor present a hazard to wildlife that might ingest them. This is an expanding problem in areas where much repetitive shooting takes place, whether a grouse moor in Scotland, a sand grouse flight in the Okavango Delta, or a quail plantation in the south.

The three major hull materials have different wall thicknesses, with paper being the thickest and brass the thinnest. Plastic walls fall somewhere in between.

Some shotshell manufacturers make completely biodegradable shotshells for use on estates, often stamped with the estate's name. They have paper cases that rot, steel cups that rust away, and fiber wads that become part of the soil. Even the shot (steel, tungsten-matrix, and bismuth), eventually rusts or disintegrates. Leaving wads and hulls littering the landscape may be only an aesthetic problem, or it may have life-threatening implications. It is an environmental concern, either way. Handloaders should at least consider this, when deciding what load and components to use for which purposes. As with legally mandated non-lead shot, you may encounter restrictions on wad types for use on public lands or private estates.

SHOT

Shot is the center around which everything else to do with shotguns revolves. These are the pellets that are launched to fly through the air and bring down a bird or a deer or smoke a clay disc.

For centuries, the only material used was lead, either pure or, later, alloyed with antimony. For centuries, no one looked for an alternative, so ideal for the purpose was this common base metal. Lead's primary virtue is its density, which gives a small pellet its momentum and penetration power. Next are its low melting point and its propensity for forming naturally into a sphere. It was always cheap and plentiful. Why look elsewhere? By the time lead's suitability was being questioned on environmental grounds, in the 1980s, the manufacturing of lead shot had been developed and refined to the point where we could buy the finest shot in the history of shooting, for pennies a pound.

The first shot was pure lead, which is very soft. This is an advantage in terms of expansion on impact, but it leaves the shot pellets vulnerable to deformation, either in storage, loading, or travelling up the bore, and an off-round pellet is virtually useless in the air. Lead shot is mass-produced in high "towers," where molten lead is poured through a grate, naturally forms into spheres that are cooled as they fall through the air, and then collected and graded at the bottom. This method dates from 1769, when it was discovered by an Englishman, William Watts.

Pouring lead into cold water produced "chilled shot," which was supposed to be slightly harder than pure lead shot. Later came antimony-hardened shot, produced by the same method. Soon, shotshells were being priced according to the grade of shot with which they were loaded. The final stage was plating lead pellets with copper or nickel, which allegedly made them more resistant to deformation, as well as provided the spheres with a smooth, slippery surface. In theory, instead of jamming together, the pellets would work like tiny ball bearings, rotating instead of flattening. It was a good sales pitch, anyway.

With the 1980s came some very dubious studies on the effects of accumulated lead shot on waterfowl, followed by regulations governing the shooting of migratory game birds with lead. The concern was that the buildup of lead pellets in swamps, deposited by millions of shots over a hundred years, was causing lead poisoning in birds that ingested them and then ground the pellets to powder in their digestive systems.

Regardless whether the initial scientific findings were valid, or whether the subsequent legislation on "non-toxic" shot saved a single bird's life or resulted in a net loss from other causes (more wounding, for instance), non-lead shot is now

POWDER

Ponsness-Warren presses are the Rolls Royces of the reloading world. This is one of their simpler models, the Duo-Matic. Like the more expensive progressive presses, the Duo-Matic resizes each hull to factory-original specifications and holds the hull tightly through every operation. The result is ammunition almost indistinguishable from new.

The Hornady Model 366 is typical of the high-quality progressive presses that produce a finished round with each stroke of the handle.

being mandated in an increasing number of applications. Some European countries have restricted lead severely or outlawed it entirely. Although not so far down that path as yet, the U.S. and many states are following suit. For instance, in Illinois, lead shot was banned at a trap club that flung its clays out over Lake Michigan. And, in South Dakota, non-toxic shot is required for hunting pheasants on state game preserves.

The initial non-toxic alternative was steel shot. In absolutely no characteristic is steel as good a material as lead, except for its "non-toxic" quality. It is not as dense, so the pellets in flight shed velocity more quickly. It cannot be melted easily nor formed naturally into pellets, which makes each pellet more expensive to produce. It does not compress, which causes potential problems on the user end, ranging from damaging choke tubes to breaking teeth if you bite down on one in a piece of duck breast meat. Deprived of the friendly qualities of lead, shotshell manufacturers have had to modify everything from hulls to wads, while gun makers have been forced to reengineer barrels and choke tubes to make them safe and fully functional with steel.

Finally—and this was a real problem for the first 20 years of steel shot's existence and one that has not disappeared even today—we have the problem of steel being unable to kill a bird as effectively as does lead. The incidence of birds wounded with steel, escaping to die slowly, while hunters continued hunting and filling their limits, was a real problem for many years. There is no way of measuring how many birds were lost this way, compared to how many were supposedly saved by the conversion from lead. After all, the lead build-up of a hundred years was still there; birds would not have miraculously stopped dying—if they were dying at all—because we suddenly stopped adding lead to the buildup.

The question of effectiveness was the most pressing for shotshell manufacturers and hunters. One way of counteracting it was to use pellets a size or two larger. If you do that, however, you have thinner patterns. So, to counteract that, you use a larger shot charge. But 1½ ounces of steel is considerably bulkier than 1¼ ounces of lead, so then the charge is packed into a longer shotshell. This was the problem that prompted the introduction of the 3½-inch 12-gauge shell by Federal Cartridge, in 1987.

A better approach was to find a nontoxic material with the positive qualities of lead. Several were tried, with bismuth one of the earliest. It is almost as heavy as lead, but it is expensive, and the pellets tend to crumble or fragment, rather than compress. Tin was loaded in England for several years, but fell just short in every measurement: not as dense, nor as malleable, nor as cheap. Tungsten is an extremely hard metal that is more dense than lead, but it is difficult to work with. Pure tungsten pellets will act on a bore like a diamond abrasive unless there is a plastic cushion in between and, even then, tungsten gave questionable patterns in early loads—which were, by the way, hideously expensive. In England, Kent Cartridge developed a pellet called "tungsten-matrix," made of ground tungsten in an adhesive. Tungsten-matrix pellets compressed, worked as well as lead in the same size pellets, and were biodegradable. The only problem was cost, which was high, with seemingly no way around it.

The final stage was Hevi-Shot, pellets made from a variety of components and manufactured and loaded in many different forms, since 2000. Denser than lead (by 10 to 30 percent, depending on the company), non-toxic in any form, its real drawback, aside from cost, is that it will not form naturally into a sphere, when in the molten state. Instead, its pellets form into teardrops, oblongs, or tiny eggs. This results in misshapen patterns. Ammunition makers have tried to turn this vice into a virtue by insisting that the long, straggling tails of shot patterns allow you to miss your birds far out in front, but catch them with the last struggling pellets of the pattern. Well, good luck. Few of us miss in front, even if we make a conscious effort to do so, and especially on a hard-flying duck. This brings us back to steel, which, in terms of cost, is still the most viable—and cost is the biggest stumbling block with non-lead shot for anyone who shoots in any volume.

Shotshell makers are now taking another look at steel and improving their shotshells, in order to make them more effective. Unfortunately, their loading methods and materials are better than the average handloader has at his disposal. Though there is now loading data, suitable wads, and steel shot available for handloaders who want or need to load their own non-lead shells, it is difficult, if not impossible, for the average guy, with his MEC press, to duplicate Kent's Fasteel or Federal's Black Cloud Steel. Since these are waterfowl loads and the average hunter does not shoot very many in a morning in the marsh, the cost of factory ammunition for hunting is not a huge barrier.

Of course, in the case of shotshells for ducks and geese, buying the least expensive or trying to save a few pennies may be self-defeating. To give a real-life example, in 2000, I hunted ducks in Manitoba's Delta Marsh, using different types of non-lead shotshells. One duck, brought down with a steel load, was swimming away as I fired nine more shells in order to bring it to a halt and allow us to get to it. Similar ducks hit with tungsten were dead where they splashed. This happened more than

once, although this was the most glaring instance. The question you have to ask is, do 10 steel shotshells cost less than one tungsten?

In the last couple years, in a marketing blitz intended to sell more factory ammunition, some makers have started pushing shot with bizarre characteristics. Since many non-lead alternatives have to be moulded anyway, there's no reason not to mould them into oddball shapes. So we now have shot with ridges or flat surfaces separated with sharp edges, like a geodesic dome or miniature disco ball. According to the hype, these edges supposedly slash through feathers and flesh, inflicting instantly mortal wounds on hapless bird life. Most of these creations are not available for handloaders, just as most non-lead alternatives have been either unavailable, hard to come by, or excruciatingly expensive. But, to be fair, it is a bit much to expect a company to put a lot of time and money into researching an alternative, set up the machinery to produce it, and then sell it to handloaders cheaply to allow them to avoid buying the ammunition.

* * *

The other projectiles most commonly ejected from the muzzle of a shotgun are slugs, for big-game hunting, and buckshot, for either hunting or self-defense.

The earliest slug was simply a round lead ball, cast in a mould like a lead bullet. They were pure lead, because pure lead would flatten on impact and impart considerable shock.

In 1998, when bismuth shot was being loaded by a company now gone from the scene, a group of writers was treated to some demonstrations of shock power, at a ranch in California. Thin steel plates were hung from hooks and then shot with different loads, identical in every way except the shot with which they were loaded. Bismuth, which flattens on impact, would knock the plate off the hooks every time, while tungsten, heavier but diamond-hard, would puncture the sheet of steel and leave it swinging gently in the breeze.

This shock power is the reason pure lead bullets were so valued for big-game hunting in the late 1800s, and this carried over to the use of round balls in shotshells, and later elongated slugs. The Foster-type slug, which was the standard for years, resembles a Minié ball, or an inverted cup, its hollow base expanding to provide a gas seal in the bore, and then the whole projectile flattening on impact. The Foster slug has slanted grooves on the sides, a sort of reverse rifling intended to cause it to spin and stabilize in flight; it is not very effective. Even so, the Foster was a quantum leap forward from the lead ball.

In Europe, Brenneke invented a two-piece slug, with the forward portion made of solid lead and having the same slanted ridges, permanently attached to a thick fiber wad that acted as a gas seal in the bore and a stabilizer in flight. The Brenneke was effective at longer ranges than the Foster and was highly prized in Africa as a leopard load.

Many years earlier, in England, Holland & Holland created a gun called the Paradox, from a patent by Lt. Col. George Vincent Fosbery, VC. The Paradox is a double-barreled shotgun with its bores rifled for the last six inches or so at the muzzle. It fires special Paradox slug loads, with the rifling imparting a spin that stabilizes the projectile far beyond the normal range of a lead ball, which is limited to about 50 yards. Other English makers followed suit with their own designs and trade names like the Fauneta and Explora (Westley Richards) or the Colindian (Charles Lancaster).

For most big-game hunting with slugs, the 12-gauge was standard. During the era when Foster slugs predominated, the 20-gauge was dismissed as a short-range, small-game proposition at best. In recent years, as more states have mandated "shotgun only" deer hunting, ammunition makers have made huge strides in the development of slugs. The great breakthrough was the "sabot," a two-piece shoe containing the actual projectile. After the bullet and sabot exit the muzzle, the sabot falls away, leaving the bullet in flight. Equipped with rifle sights and rifled barrels that grip the sabot and impart spin, such shotguns are more effective than many big-game rifles of a hundred years ago, and increase the effective range of a shotgun to several hundred yards.

All this rather defeats the purpose of the shotguns-only regulations, which were supposed to limit the long-range hazards associated with rifles, but that's their problem. Such state of the art loads are expensive, but a deer hunter with a shotgun fires no more ammunition than a rifle hunter and frequently much less, since a shotgun does not do multiple duty with slug loads. It is rarely economic to try to save money by handloading these particular loads. As well, it is difficult to match the performance, and that is vital in big-game hunting.

Aside from Federal, Winchester, and Remington, many small ammunition makers have plunged into this smooth-bore arms race, with slug designs that range from logical to bizarre. One design resembled the old Foster, but the slug was striated, designed to break into three large chunks on impact, each flying a different direction into the animal's vitals. This introduces an element of haphazard chance that may not be reassuring, if you are hunting a leopard in thick bush. Some of these creations are available to handloaders, others are not.

Before the slug there was buckshot, so called because it was larger than birdshot and used for hunting bucks. Buckshot has a fearsome reputation, and it loses nothing in the movie depictions of hapless bad guys, picked up and thrown through windows by the impact of a double load of buckshot. In Africa, a 12-bore loaded with buckshot in each barrel was, for years, the recommended weapon, when going after a wounded cat. Wally Johnson, the famous Mozambique professional hunter, is widely quoted as saying that, when faced with a wounded lion, a hunter with a double load of SSG (the English designation for 00 Buckshot) was "as safe as a babe in its crib."

Now let's get to reality, and not so as to contradict Wally Johnson; he was correct within certain limits, but few writers bother to explain what those limits are. The corollary to the "babe in its crib" rule is that you must be cool enough to let the beast get within 10 yards before shooting. Out to 10 yards, the shot charge is still in a clump, not yet expanding, and strikes the animal with the force of a slug. At 20 yards, when the pellets have separated into a shot cloud, they have considerably less force, and what there is is diminishing rapidly. In such a situation, attempting to hit the animal with what is essentially one projectile, rather than a cloud of pellets, why not use the vastly more effective slug? Very likely, it was because slugs were not available. Such is not the case today.

Some years ago, I experimented shooting plastic jugs of water with different guns and loads at 20 yards. A one-gallon jug, perched on a post, makes a most impressive display when struck by a .257 Weatherby, a .500 Nitro Express, or a load of buck. The .257 destroyed the jug and vaporized the water; the .500 turned

This is the slug produced by Polywad. On impact, it is designed to break into three equal parts, each of which penetrates in a different direction. This is just one of the innovative approaches to slug design brought about by increased mandating of shotguns for deer hunting.

the jug to shards and the water to rain. The load of buckshot—Federal 000, eight .36-inch pellets to the load—left the jug sitting contentedly on the post with eight sedate streams of water pouring from eight holes, like a Roman fountain. Further tests on a penetration box packed with soaked newsprint showed just how ragged are the patterns and how limited was the penetration of individual buckshot pellets.

At best, buckshot is an extremely short-range proposition, 20 to 30 yards, 40 at the outside. In the South, buckshot was used in the traditional deer drives of the early twentieth century. There, a buck running along a trail would come within a few yards of the gun. In Europe, it is used today in shooting driven boar,

which also come within a few yards. The long-range ineffectiveness of buckshot becomes a virtue, because it drastically reduces danger to spectators or other hunters. There are, of course, exceptions to everything. Someone might have a shotgun they load with buck and, with certain loads and chokes, get a tight pattern out to 75 yards. Unless the law requires buckshot, however, most shotgun-only big-game hunting situations are far better served with slugs.

The other real application of buckshot today is for tactical shotguns, where limiting range and penetration is desirable. It also finds a suitable home with some competitions, such as those Cowboy Action Shooting participants.

CHAPTER 7

BLACKPOWDER SHOTGUNS

Blackpowder shotguns come in all forms and configurations, from muzzleloader and pinfires to centerfire cartridge guns. Joseph Manton's masterpieces from the early 1800s were first flintlock muzzleloaders and, later, caplock (or percussion) muzzleloaders. These established the form and principles of the modern fowling piece. Muzzleloaders are outside the scope of this book, but they are the starting point from which everything else flows. Today, many shotgunners enjoy hunting and shooting with all kinds of blackpowder shotguns, some old, others new reproductions of old designs.

Although blackpowder might be considered old fashioned or outdated, it can be almost as effective today as it was in the 1800s—and that was very effective indeed. In fact, in the early days of smokeless powder, there were many who clung to blackpowder for certain uses in which it was actually more effective than smokeless.

The transition from blackpowder to smokeless was not instant; with shotguns in England, it took place over the course of 20 to 30 years. Smokeless shotgun powders preceded smokeless rifle powders by a good number of years, but even by the 1890s, when smokeless powder was taking over in military rifles and cartridges, and smokeless shotgun powders had been largely perfected, many still preferred blackpowder and used it for one purpose, smokeless for another. Today, blackpowder cartridges are still loaded commercially and lend themselves admirably to the art of

Writer Garry James with a sharptail grouse, taken with his vintage Westley Richards hammer gun.

wingshooting, where high velocity is not required and ranges are reasonable.

A muzzleloader is charged by pouring powder down the barrel, following it with a wad to keep it in place, pouring a charge of shot on top of the wad, and following that with another wad to keep the shot firmly in place. Generally, barrels were long, 30 inches at least, and often longer. This length was required to fully exploit the power of the powder charge.

The idea of creating a gun that would load from the breech, rather than the muzzle, dates back at least to the 1700s. From 1800 to 1850, a wide variety of methods were attempted. Some were dead

Trimming paper cases to length for use in guns with shorter chambers.

Some of the fibre wads used for loading blackpowder shotshells.

ends, while others led to further developments. There were a number of interrelated problems. These included perfecting a usable mechanism for opening and closing the gun, a design for a self-contained cartridge, a means of ignition, and some way of sealing the breech against escaping gases.

Swiss gun maker Samuel Johannes Pauly patented a breechloading gun with a self-contained cartridge, in 1812. French gun makers seized on the concept and, from there, the pursuit of a practical, usable breechloading mechanism continued in France, while the more conservative British gun makers stuck with muzzleloading percussion guns and brought their manufacture to a level of high art.

A number of patents taken out through the 1830s and '40s covered the major aspects of a workable shotgun with a self-contained cartridge. By 1851, Paris gun maker Casimir Lefaucheux had developed the break-action gun, in which the barrels pivoted to open the breech and employing

a pinfire cartridge in which an expanding base wad sealed the breech against escaping gas. These were not all Lefaucheux's inventions and patents, but Lefaucheux put it all together and exhibited two of his creations at London's Great Exhibition of 1851. This watershed event set off the breechloading era in English shotguns.

The pinfire was the first truly successful breechloading shotgun. The pinfire shotshell resembles a modern cartridge, except that, instead of an external primer, there is an internal one with a long pin extending at a right angle out of the base. The cartridge is inserted with the pin pointing up; a tiny notch in the barrel face accommodates the pin, and the breech cannot be closed with the pin out of position. This pin is struck by the falling hammer, much like the cap on a caplock. The pin detonates the internal cap charged with priming compound, and this, in turn, ignites the blackpowder in the case.

The pinfire era in England lasted from the mid-1850s into the 1870s and estab-

Turning the crimp on paper hulls, using a nineteenth-century "turn-over" tool.

lished the form of the classic side-by-side shotgun. Pinfire cartridges were almost always reloaded, and brass pinfire cases last indefinitely, if not abused.

The step from the pinfire to the centerfire shotshell, also a French development (like the break-action shotgun itself), which was introduced to England by gun maker George Daw, took place in the 1860s. Since it was easy to convert a gun from pinfire to centerfire, many owners of Lancaster, Woodward, Purdey, and other fine pinfires had them converted, rather than buy a new gun. Partly for this reason, there are relatively few pinfires for sale compared to early centerfires.

Like blackpowder itself, pinfires hung on long after they had been displaced by centerfires for everyday use. Pinfire guns are very durable, so there was a continuing demand for ammunition, and pinfire shotshells were available until at least the 1930s. The guns themselves, being considered obsolete by mainstream shooters, sold for pennies on the pound. English shotgun writer G.T. Garwood (Gough Thomas), wrote about beginning his shooting career, in the 1920s, with an old pinfire shotgun. It was all he could afford with an engineering student's available cash, but it taught him a great deal about shotguns and shooting, and he retained great affection for them. The other small contingent of shooting gentlemen with pinfire guns who refused to convert them continued to shoot them for years, because the loads were effective and the guns handled to perfection.

In 1872, Sir Frederick Milbank, Bart., delivered one of the most astonishing wingshooting performances of all time. On August 20, on Wemmergill Moor, he downed 728 red grouse in eight drives. He was shooting a trio of Westley Richards pinfire guns and employed two loaders. His load was 7/8-ounce of No. 6 (American No. 7) shot over 2½ drams of blackpowder. Muzzle velocity was 1,100 feet per second.

A hammer gun by J. Woodward & Sons, circa 1900, with a wild South Dakota pheasant taken with blackpowder. It was highly effective then, and it's highly effective now.

Blackpowder has its own charms.

Factory ammunition loaded with blackpowder is still available from some manufacturers, such as this Gamebore ammunition from England. The gun (also on the previous page) is a Woodward.

The red grouse is a big, wild, hard-flying bird, and shooting driven red grouse is the toughest assignment in wingshooting. By 1872, centerfire cartridges had largely crowded out pinfires. In fact, both hammerless centerfire guns and the early smokeless powders were already looming on the horizon. Yet Sir Frederick stuck to his Westley Richards pinfires and blackpowder cartridges, because they were so effective for him and he was so effective shooting them.

This is a good place to deal with the question of drams (or drachms) and gunpowder measurement. The dram is most famously used in connection with blackpowder and Scotch whisky ("a wee dram"), and outside of certain apothecary shops, that is where it is found today. The dram hung on long after smokeless powder displaced blackpowder in most applications, and it appears on shotshell boxes today in the words "dram equivalent" or

"Dr. Eq.," as explained in the previous chapter. For a century, shotshell velocities were indicated by this term, which denotes an amount of smokeless powder that is the equivalent of a dram of blackpowder. The dram itself is a unit of both mass (weight) and volume, and there is a liquid dram as well (hence the Scotch). In weight, a dram is $1/16$-ounce, or 27 grains.

It should be obvious that one dram of blackpowder will propel a lighter load of shot at a higher velocity than it will a heavier one, so the term is less an indication of actual velocity than it is relative power. Even today, when many shotshell boxes display measured muzzle velocity, they still include dram equivalent, because it means something to many shooters. Eventually it will disappear, but, when it does, an interesting facet of shotgun shooting will disappear with it.

Blackpowder shooters today measure powder either by grains or bulk measure-

Components for loading a blackpowder ball for a 20-bore hammer gun.

Seating the over-powder wad in a 20-bore brass hull.

Crimping the mouth using a vintage (and rare) bronze Kynoch crimping tool.

Twenty-bore ball loads ready for crimping.

ment. With blackpowder, it is more important to fill available space, leaving no air pockets, than it is to get the exact weight of powder. In this regard, blackpowder is much more forgiving than the faster-burning smokeless shotshell powders.

Pinfire cases are still available in different shotshell sizes, and reloading kits can be purchased for them. Centerfire blackpowder cartridges are commonly reloaded, because factory ammunition is expensive. Added to that, since blackpowder is classed as an explosive by the U.S. government, the ammunition is more expensive to ship. If you have a vintage shotgun, it is fun to load for it, using paper or brass cases and equally vintage loading equipment.

One caution must be added for anyone intending to load blackpowder cartridges and hoping to duplicate performances from years past. The blackpowder available today is not as good as the powder used in the 1880s. The powder acknowledged to be the best available in the 1880s was Curtis's &

Harvey's No. 6 (Extra Strength). Cartridges loaded with it were tested using the first chronographs, which were very accurate, as well as various penetration tests that were popular in England. Results from modern reloads using Goex and imported blackpowders simply don't attain those velocities.

In a world where we are accustomed to looking at modern products and proclaiming their superiority, this may sound surprising, but it's true. When you consider it, it should not be. In those days, there were many types of blackpowder on the market, it was in common use, and competition was fierce among powder manufacturers to have their products loaded by both famous commercial ammunition makers and gun makers, as well as by home loaders. As with any field where there is intense competition, products improved and losers fell by the wayside.

Today, we are forced to make do with what we can get. In fairness to Goex, Elephant, Graf's Schuetzen, and various other European powders, they deliver good

The Kynoch crimping tool and finished round (20-bore ball).

Paper hulls are by far the best (and some consider the only) hulls to use with blackpowder. These 20-gauge paper hulls are not easy to come by.

Cast slugs for the 20-bore.

The author shooting an E.M. Reilly 20-bore hammer gun from the 1870s that began life as a .577 Snider double rifle, travelled the world for more than a century, and was later bored out to become a 20-gauge shotgun. At close range, it is deadly with ball, buck-, or birdshot.

performance and are readily available. Too, powder quality is not the only factor affecting today's performance of blackpowder, compared to that of 120 years ago. Primers are different, cases and case capacity are not the same, and wads are often made up from whatever we can find, rather than cut from prime feltine or natural cork.

If there is one serious problem with blackpowder, it is cleaning and corrosion. Blackpowder is unapologetically messy. It leaves hands black and bores coated in a greasy residue. When you get home from shooting, you need to clean your gun immediately or risk corrosion. The same is true of brass shotshells. Left uncleaned, brass shotshells deteriorate and become brittle, while blackpowder residue left in the bore or coating the standing breech may lead to rust and pitting.

The problem as it exists today is not exactly what it was in the 1860s, because the chemical compounds used for priming are not the same as they were then. The major concern now is chemical reactions among these different compounds. Since no one can predict exactly what will happen when primer "A" ignites powder "B," the safest course is to clean immediately and clean thoroughly. Fortunately, the main cleaning agent for blackpowder is soap and water, which, together, takes care of both grease and salt compounds. A fouled bore can be rendered clean as a whistle with little more than a basin of hot water, some dish detergent, and a cleaning rod and mop. You do not need to buy expensive blackpowder solvents, which seem to consist mostly of detergent anyway. Once the black grime is out of the barrel, ensure that it is absolutely dry and then apply

Blackpowder 20-bore loads for a variety of purposes, some sporting, some not.

A German pinfire gun with ammunition made by Bob Hayley (Hayley's Custom Ammunition), from modern centerfire brass hulls. Pinfires are always loaded with blackpowder.

a thin coat of oil. Much the same process will do for brass cartridge cases (except for applying oil, of course). Paper cases do not need to be cleaned, because the powder residue does not come into contact with anything that can corrode, and paper cases are generally worn out after two or three firings anyway.

Entire books have been devoted to the care and feeding of blackpowder firearms of all kinds, and anyone interested in shooting blackpowder should acquire one and read it carefully. The *Lyman Blackpowder Handbook* is a comprehensive guide to every facet of loading and shooting blackpowder. The main thing to remember, even if you are an experienced handloader accustomed to using smokeless powder, is that blackpowder is an explosive. Although it creates lower pressures and is more forgiving in the gun itself, blackpowder outside the gun—in canisters, powder measures, or open cartridges—is more volatile and hazardous than smokeless. Makers of old loading implements avoided the use of steel wherever possible, because of the possibility of sparks. The main materials used were brass and German silver. Static electricity is an equal hazard, to say nothing of cigarette ash.

* * *

There are mixed views on blackpowder and plastic, whether used in hulls, shot cups, or wads. Some say they work perfectly well, others that the ignition of blackpowder will melt or soften plastic, leading to serious plastic fouling in the bore. Unless you have no choice in your use of components, my suggestion would be to avoid the use of plastic, and not just because of the possibility of fouling. Garry James, former editor of *Guns & Ammo*

Modern blackpowders, from Germany (left, imported by Graf & Sons) and America. Goex is part of the Hodgdon Powders conglomerate.

Vintage loading tools, still eminently useful today.

and a serious devotee of blackpowder, is of the opinion that any gun or rifle made for blackpowder should be shot only with blackpowder, not with any equivalent smokeless propellant or blackpowder substitute. This is partly a matter of correct form and the rightness of things (which, of course, is a personal matter for everyone), but also because that was what they were made to shoot and shooting anything else raises the risk of damaging the gun or altering its shooting qualities.

With English or European guns, which have been specifically proofed with blackpowder and not with any nitro (smokeless) powder, it is certainly safer to stick with blackpowder. By the way, the normal term for smokeless powder proof is "nitro proof," and the word "nitro" stamped on the barrel or action flats is an indication of this. Just because a gun has been proofed with blackpowder only does *not* mean it is not safe to use smokeless powders in

prudent loads, only that the proof house has not said it is.

During the transition from blackpowder to smokeless, both rifle and shotgun ammunition were produced that were termed "smokeless for black." These were cartridges loaded with certain smokeless powders to blackpowder pressures and intended for guns proofed only for blackpowder. In the United States, some early smokeless powders were produced that were intended for the same purpose and were measured by their bulk, not by weight. The use of "bulk shotgun" powders continued until well into the twentieth century and, as late as the 1960s, shotgun writers referred to loads using bulk powders.

As you can see, there are many grey areas between the use of blackpowder and smokeless, and this is ground that must be trod carefully if you have an old shotgun and want to shoot it. There are tens of thousands of perfectly good guns, rang-

This old powder measure can be set to measure powder from 2½ to 5 drams.

ing in age from 100 to 150 years old, that can be shot, hunted with, and generally enjoyed in perfect safety and with very satisfying performance, provided they are given the right loads. This is, of course, also provided the owner does not fall prey to the modern disease of seeking to push performance to the limit, packing in more powder and shot and trying hotter primers to get more velocity in an effort to show up the other guy and *his* old gun.

It is good to keep in mind that, with a shotgun, pattern is everything. Some fine old blackpowder shotguns were carefully bored and choked to deliver exemplary patterns with a particular load and a specified number of blackpowder drams. Load them accordingly, and you will get lovely performance. Try to step outside those boundaries and you run the risk of ruining patterns or worse. Perhaps, though, this is not really a problem, since the big challenge for modern blackpowder shotgunners is merely equal-

ing the wonderful performance of these guns in 1880, rather than exceeding it.

* * *

In 1905, one of the less well-known British shooting writers, Alexander Innes Shand, wrote about the transition from muzzleloaders to breechloading shotguns, regretting the fact that modern shooters were relatively ignorant about their firearms. In the days of blackpowder, when it was necessary to dismantle a gun every time you returned home to check its mechanism and clean and oil the bore, every shooter, whether lord or gamekeeper or vicar, knew a great deal about his gun and how it worked. In modern times, with its non-fouling ammunition, Shand wrote that too many shooters ignore their gun as much as possible and, as a result, really know very little about them.

In the intervening 108 years, this situation has become a thousand times worse.

Blackpowder paper, from Gamebore, in glossy hulls of rifle green.

Because modern powders and primers are non-corrosive and newer steels and alloys used in shotguns are either rust-free or corrosion-proof, it is hardly necessary ever to clean a shotgun and, so, many do not.

You must know, though, that, when you take up blackpowder shooting, it requires a complete change of attitude, one from regarding your gun as an inanimate object that requires little or no attention nearly to the status of a pet that requires daily care and constant observation. Left to themselves, old blackpowder guns seem almost to attract rust and fouling. If you cannot afford the time or don't want to make gun care a labor of love and an adjunct pleasurable activity to the shooting itself, then perhaps blackpowder is not for you. If, on the other hand, you love to sit by a fire and read about the great shoots of the nineteenth century, to sip a little single malt and reflect on life as a laird, to take a quiet hour to spend with your gun and a bottle of Rangoon oil, then very likely you would find yourself right at home in the world of blackpowder shotguns.

CHAPTER 8

SHOTGUN GAMES

S hotgun competition is one of the oldest of all sports still in existence. It began in Europe in the 1700s, and the first recorded events occurred in England, in 1792, almost 25 years before Wellington defeated Napoleon at the Battle of Waterloo.

THE PIGEON IN HISTORY

The first competitions were live-pigeon shooting events, in which captured birds were released and shot under controlled conditions. From the beginning, pigeon shooting involved betting, and sometimes very substantial sums of money. Not coincidentally, this was the era of the Manton brothers, John and Joseph, who are credited with turning the fowling piece from a crude implement into a refined tool. This evolution was due in no small part to pigeon shooting.

Up until then, fine gun making had been limited to dueling pistols. Taking a cue from the importance of such firearms needing to be dependable in the heat of the moment, gun makers like Manton and, later, Lancaster and Purdey understood that, when hundreds of pounds were at stake, having a gun that was utterly dependable, fit properly, and was well balanced could be the difference between survival and bankruptcy. It was many years before other game guns caught up to pigeon guns in sophistication and workmanship.

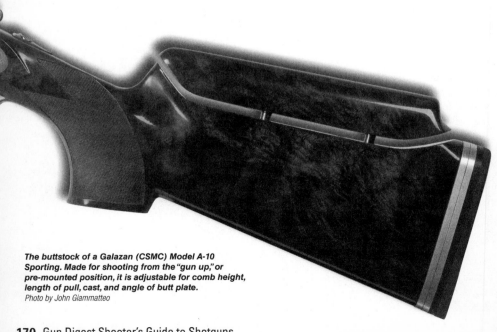

The buttstock of a Galazan (CSMC) Model A-10 Sporting. Made for shooting from the "gun up," or pre-mounted position, it is adjustable for comb height, length of pull, cast, and angle of butt plate.
Photo by John Giammatteo

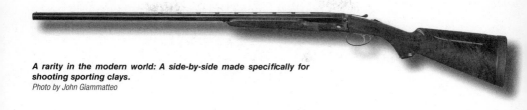

A rarity in the modern world: A side-by-side made specifically for shooting sporting clays.
Photo by John Giammatteo

There are various types of pigeon shooting, but the two in existence today are "box pigeon" and *columbaire.*

In box-pigeon shooting, the birds are held in boxes (traps), five in a line and five yards apart from each other. The shooter stands 29 yards back from the center trap, calls for a bird, and one is released at random from one of the five traps. The bird then must be downed, "grassed" is the term, inside a fenced ring surrounding the field. Shooters are awarded handicaps that determine whether they stand at the 29-yard line or farther back in one-yard increments back to 35 yards.

In *columbaire,* the pigeon is thrown by hand, rather than released from a trap. Most widely practiced in South America, this is really a contest between the *columbaire* (thrower) and the shooter, much like a duel between a pitcher and a batter, in baseball. The throwing ring is square, outlined by a surrounding rope 10 feet above the ground. Another rope divides the square into two rectangles. The thrower is in one rectangle, the shooter in the other, and both can move within their respective rectangles. The bird must be thrown over the rope in any direction. As in box-pigeon shooting, the bird must be downed inside a fenced, circular ring, otherwise it is counted as lost.

In the early years in Europe, shooting clubs used starlings, sparrows, and other birds, when pigeons were not available. Pigeons were expensive, so pigeon shooting became a big-money competition in every way. Then, as pigeons became either too costly or unobtainable, various kinds of artificial targets were created. This is the origin of trap shooting, the oldest shooting game involving artificial targets.

Because of the need not only to kill the bird, but also to drop it within an enclosed area, pigeon guns have tight chokes and hard-hitting loads. Guns and loads for pigeon shooting eventually became standardized. Upper limits were placed on both shot loads and powder charges. Rules were also established that limited gauge sizes.

Box-pigeon guns are very high quality, and this is the root of the "pigeon grade" often associated with shotguns. Eventually, the standard charge for a pigeon load became "1¼ - 3¼"—that is, 1¼ ounces of shot, propelled by 3¼ drams of black-powder. Pigeon guns were heavier than standard weight, to absorb recoil, and had long barrels and tight chokes. In England, they were chambered for 2¾-inch shotshells and often had heftier frames with features like third bites and side clips, for additional strength and stability.

Columbaire guns more closely resemble game guns. The first shot is generally at closer range, and the first barrel has a more open choke. These guns are still heavy, however, to absorb the recoil of the substantial load.

In both games, the shooter is allowed two shots at each bird and, in some instances, required by the rules to fire both barrels regardless. Pigeon guns are always doubles, traditionally side-by-sides, but, in more recent years, over/unders, as well.

The author in practice for the real thing, in this case, shooting clays coming at random off a hill top. He is working with a "stuffer."

Unlike trap and skeet, where hundreds of shots are fired in a day of competition, pigeon shooting involves much smaller numbers. A 30-bird "race" is typical for a day's shoot, with 15 birds in the morning and 15 in the afternoon. A two-day shoot would total 60 birds. This means there is much more care and deliberation taken with each shot, and the pace is much slower. Pigeon shooting is much more difficult, shot for shot, than trap. Even the very finest pigeon shooters rarely kill 30 birds in a row and, in a 60-bird match, the winning score is very likely to be 56 or 57 grassed birds.

An interesting aspect of pigeon shooting is that the shooters are absolutely top-flight. Many turn to pigeon shooting, because they had conquered all the fields that trap had to offer. At the same time, and although there are substantial purses on the line, the atmosphere is unfailingly friendly and congenial, unlike the cutthroat (and sometimes neurotic), world of trap.

TRAP SHOOTING

The modern sport of trap shooting came about for two reasons, the expense of live-pigeon shooting and objections to it on humanitarian grounds.

The development that made trap shooting possible was the invention of the round clay disc, in 1880, patented by the American George Ligowsky. Until that time, various types of targets had been tried, including glass balls, balls filled with feathers, and wooden cubes. All had drawbacks. Some didn't present enough of a challenge, others created too much litter. The clay target was the breakthrough that made trap shooting possible.

Trap's layout, procedures, rules, and terminology all flow from box-pigeon shooting, with the exception of the fact that,

Blaser gun maker Andre Gorjup adjusting the stock of competitor Alison Caselman's Blaser F3 tournament gun.

instead of competitors shooting individually, one at a time, shooters compete in squads of five, each firing one shot in turn and rotating back through the line, in turn, until all have fired the full game.

The term "trap" comes from pigeon shooting, as does the clay "pigeon." (In England, trap shooting is called "down the line" or DTL, to differentiate it from pigeon shooting.)

The traditional call of "Pull!" originated with pulling a cord to open a trap and release a bird, and the machine that launches clay pigeons is called a "trap." The trademark Blue Rock of some clays actually comes from blue rock pigeons, the favored species for live-pigeon shooting.

In trap shooting, the trap itself is housed in a sunken building 16 yards in front of the line of shooters. The trap oscillates from side to side, out of sight of the guns. When the shooter calls "Pull!" the trap releases the bird at whatever angle the oscillating trap is pointing at the time, which gives a variety of shots ranging from hard lefts to straightaways to hard rights, and these angles change as shooters rotate from station No. 1 through station No. 5. Each shooter gets five shots at each station, then moves to the next, to shoot a total of 25 for the match.

As an interesting side note, our own famous Grand American trap shooting championship originally used live pigeons. The last live-pigeon competition was held in 1902. Since then, the Grand has been clay pigeon only.

Trap guns are the most specialized of all shotguns, and the game itself has been referred to as rifle shooting with a shotgun. Trap is shot with 12-gauge guns; while there is no rule against using a smaller gauge, there are no special classes, and no allowance is given for using one.

The clays are broken at anywhere from 32 to 45 yards, depending how quickly the gun gets on the bird, and, so, trap guns are long-barreled, heavy, and tightly choked. Because 16-yard trap is shot one clay at a time, the single-barrel trap gun became an American specialty, with superb guns produced by Parker, L.C. Smith and, most famous of all, Ithaca. The legendary Ithaca Single remained on the market right up until the 1980s, in production long after Ithaca doubles had been abandoned. Today, fine single-barrel trap guns are produced by Browning and Perazzi.

In trap, the gun is mounted to the shoulder, with the safety off, before the shooter calls for the bird. Because of this, trap guns have long, straight stocks, with Monte Carlo (raised) combs, and beavertail or oversized fore-ends that provide a firm grip. The guns are heavy, typically nine to 9½ pounds. Traditionally, single-barrel dedicated trap guns have no safety, because they are never loaded until it is the shooter's turn.

By game gun standards, trap loads are relatively light—no more than $1\frac{1}{8}$ ounces of shot at moderate velocities—and trap guns themselves are heavy. The damaging effects of recoil, especially the development of a flinch, is cumulative, with many light loads having as bad an effect as a few heavy loads. Trap shooters fear a flinch above all things, because hesitation in pulling the trigger inevitably means a lost bird. This is a game where runs of 100 straight are common, and the loss of even one bird means an early exit from competition.

There are many variations on trap. Handicap trap moves shooters back as far as 27 yards from the trap house, to increase difficulty, and handicap loads are more powerful than standard shells. A shooter's handicap is determined by his record in registered competition. Doubles trap follows the same basic format, except two birds are thrown each time. The doubles trap does not oscillate. Instead, variation in the targets is achieved by the shooters rotating through the five stations, thereby seeing the targets from

Alison Caselman at low house No. 7 on the skeet range. The other members of the team are watching where the clay will break. Alison's gun is pre-mounted and pointed to where the clay will be, not where it is.

Trap shooting from the 16-yard line, as seen from beyond the trap.

Another angle on a trap-shooting layout.

Yet another angle on trap. Most trap layouts overlay a skeet field, allowing the club to make maximum use of available space, hence the view of the skeet high house, although the team is preparing to shoot trap.

Preparing to shoot trap. The view from behind the shooters.

different angles. A standard round of doubles trap is 50 shots, instead of 25.

* * *

During the 1980s and '90s, as sporting clays roared to popularity, trap shooting saw a decline in interest. Partly this was due to the intense regulation of every as-pect of it, and partly it was due to the fact that perfect scores had become the norm and many high-level matches had become endurance contests, as much as anything. Sporting clays offered variety, a change of pace, and new challenges for shooters.

A side effect of this decline in interest in the game of trap was that very high-

Another view of trap.

quality used trap guns became available at bargain prices. This was particularly true in the state of Arizona, because legend had it that Arizona was where old trap shooters went to die. For many years, you could hardly give away the old classic single-barrel trap guns. Today, the pendulum has swung back in the other direction, largely because of collegiate shooting. For college teams and young shooters, trap is the perfect game. Fields are available, they are identical, a score shot on one corresponds to another, it lends itself to team participation, and competitors can see exactly where they stand in intercollegiate competition. As a result of this renewed interest, there has also been an upsurge in new trap guns. Almost all are over/under doubles, although some also offer an interchangeable single-barrel.

Not surprisingly, with a game as old as trap—it has been an Olympic event since 1900—there are variations found in different parts of the world, and even from club to club. One is known as "wobble trap," a game in which the trap oscillates up and down, as well as side to side. Others include allowing two shots at each bird and scoring more (or less) for each break, depending on whether it was hit with the first or second shot. Anyone shooting trap at a new club should check for any local rules or peculiarities, especially as they regard guns, safeties, allowed shots, and chambering cartridges.

INTERNATIONAL TRAP

International, Olympic, or bunker trap is the usual game shot outside the U.S., and, until in very recent years, there was only one true international setup in the entire country. Today there are several, as well as modified 16-yard trap fields that allow for a simulation of international competition. While Olympic trap has the same origins as American trap, it has grown into quite a different game and is generally considered to be much more difficult and demanding than 16-yard trap.

An international field has five stations for shooters and employs five sets of three traps each. There is a set of traps below each station, one pointing left, one right, and one straight. Instead of shooting five birds at each station before moving, each shooter in this game moves after each shot. To save time, a squad consists of six shooters, with the sixth

The bird is in the air, approximately 32 yards out (and fleeing fast).

moving from station No. 5 back to behind station No. 1 after each shot. This keeps the game moving.

The traps do *not* move. They are computer-programmed to throw each shooter a total of 25 birds—10 right, 10 left, five straight-away—but in a random sequence. The computer keeps track of which shooter is at which station and which birds he or she has already seen. A standard round is 125 shots for men, 75 for women. The targets are thrown at a much higher speed than in American trap (62 miles per hour, versus 40). Originally, the gun was held below the shoulder, rather than mounted, and two shots were allowed at each bird. Olympic competition now allows only one shot. The maximum shot charge is also regulated, with 24 grams ($^7/_8$-ounce) the maximum allowed, but at higher velocities of 1,400 to 1,500 fps.

International trap layouts are very expensive and, until relatively recently, only one existed in the entire United States. Even today they are rare. To provide practice for aspiring Olympic shooters, some trap clubs have created simulated interna-

tional fields, allowing two shots per clay, setting the traps to throw harder targets, and rearranging stations and trap houses so the shooter is above the trap. Because international trap shooters fire two shots in rapid succession, there is a premium on speed and reduced recoil. Emphasis is placed on getting the shot out to the fleeing target as quickly as possible.

SKEET

From its beginnings, trap shooting was intended to simulate live-pigeon shooting and had no relation whatever to game shooting. As trap became more and more formal and rigid and its guns more specialized, hunters began looking for an alternative that would provide practice in the off-season for hunting grouse, pheasants, and other game birds later in the fall.

The answer was skeet, a game formalized in the U.S., in 1926, and named for the Norse word for "shoot." The moniker was suggested in a national name-the-game contest won by a lady named Gertrude Hurlbutt. Miss Hurlbutt went on to become one of the foremost female skeet shooters of her day.

Skeet is quite unlike trap in every way except the clay pigeons themselves. There are eight shooting stations laid out in a semicircle, numbered from one to seven. There are two trap houses, one throwing a high bird, the other throwing a low bird. Station No. 1 is directly beneath the high-house trap, station No. 7 beside the low house. Station No. 8, the last shooting station, is halfway between the two houses, on the straight line between them.

The traps themselves are fixed in position and do not move at all, throwing each bird exactly the same. Ideally, every bird thrown from each trap will be identical in flight. The only variety is the angle provided by the movement of the shooter from station to station. Birds are shot in singles and doubles, depending on the station, and a round of skeet is 25 shots. On the double stations, one high bird and one low bird cross in the air.

The low house at skeet, with the team on station No. 7.

In skeet, the average bird is broken around 22 yards, so skeet guns have little or no choke. A typical skeet gun might have 26- or 28-inch barrels, choked Skeet No. 1 and Skeet No. 2, both of which are close to Improved Cylinder. Unlike trap, which is strictly a 12-gauge game, skeet is shot with 12-, 20-, and 28-gauge, and .410-bore guns, and a registered match includes rounds shot with all four.

Originally, skeet was shot with the gun down and the safety on. After the call "Pull!" the gun was brought to the shoulder and the safety slipped off as the gun was raised. Today, American skeet is shot, like trap, with the gun mounted and the safety off. As a result, new skeet guns more closely resemble trap guns than game guns, with long barrels, thick fore-ends, and Monte Carlo stocks.

Ryan Mason on a simulated ruffed-grouse station of a sporting clays range. Sporting clays offers a virtually unlimited variety of conditions and terrain.

Sporting clays can be varied by adding different levels to the shooting platform. Here, Alison Caselman shoots a flushing grouse from the high platform.

Just as trap and skeet are quite unlike one another, so, too, are trap shooters different than skeet shooters. Arguments continue as to which game is the more difficult. Trap has the element of the unexpected built into each target by its oscillating trap, and this factor gives trap the edge on difficulty. In skeet, while there are eight stations, two traps, and 20 different presentations, in the end, they are exactly alike, without deviation, time after time. Trap rounds are like snowflakes, whereas every skeet round is exactly like every other skeet round.

Originating in the Northeast, stations in skeet were intended to simulate the various flight patterns of the ruffed grouse, and the first skeet guns were typical grouse guns. As the rules became more defined, shooting more formalized, and national associations began to keep records and regulate tournaments, skeet guns became more specialized. Particularly, because of the requirement to shoot four gauges in registered tournaments, skeet guns were produced with interchangeable barrels in the four gauges. Today, the skeet gun is as specialized as the trap or pigeon gun.

Skeet loads closely resemble trap loads, the main difference being the pellet size. In trap, No. 7½ is standard, while skeet shooters use No. 9s.

INTERNATIONAL SKEET

International skeet is similar to international trap in that the birds fly faster, the

Looking back at the flushing-grouse shooting platform. It offers a variety of shooting angles, both horizontal and vertical.

Alison on a simulated duck station, overlooking a pond with cattails and surrounding trees.

regulations call for the gun to be held off the shoulder until the bird is called for, and the presentations at each station are more difficult. Anyone shooting international skeet for the first time is likely to be caught flat-footed on the first few targets. Reaction time is all important. As with international trap loads, special ammunition for international skeet uses a smaller charge of shot at higher velocities.

SPORTING CLAYS

The game we now call sporting clays originated in England, in the 1920s, although informal variations existed at different shooting grounds well before that. It was developed as an artificial target game to give practice for game shooting.

The English shooting grounds, complete with practice targets and professional instruction, dates back to the 1870s. Different grounds installed target stations that simulated the various shots you were likely to see in the field while hunting game, everything from bounding rabbits and incoming grouse to high pheasants launched off a tower. Some shooting grounds put in "grouse butts," actual shooting butts sunk into the ground, with clays thrown at them in twos, threes, and packs, completely at random. Today, these are run by computer programs and offer 50- or 100-shot flurries. With a loader and two guns, it is more fun than can be imagined.

It was a short step from these practice stations to entire courses, stringing together eight or 10 stations, shooting 50 to 100

Ryan Mason, shooting birds off the high tower at Prairie Grove Shooting Sports, near Columbia, Missouri. The tower is 90 feet high, with more than a dozen traps throwing birds in every direction from 10 different levels. Although towers have been common in England for many years, they have only really made an appearance in the U.S. in the last 25 years or so. They offer a tremendous variety of shots at all heights and angles, including incoming, crossing, and outgoing.

cartridges per round. Originally, they were to be shot with standard game guns, which were held gun down, safety on, exactly as one would approach a point over a dog or wait for an incoming grouse.

The first sporting clays course in the U.S. was set up near Houston, in 1984, by Bryan Bilinski, who then worked for Orvis and now has a gun shop in Traverse City, Michigan. By 1984, both trap and skeet were losing popularity. Trap was seen as an old man's game, shot with archaic guns, a game repetitive and formal, with little or no relevance to game shooting. Skeet wasn't much better, shot by rote, with runs of consecutive breaks into the thousands. Shooters were bored.

Americans took to sporting clays with joyous cries, and new clays courses spread throughout the country like dandelions in spring. By the mid-1990s, everyone seemed to be shooting sporting, and the first dedicated sporting clays guns were coming onto the market. The popularity of sporting clays was credited with keeping the gun manufacturers solvent for more than a decade, and there was a vigorous revival in the shotgun market, as a result.

As a game, sporting clays was supposed to present realistic game-shooting situations, from incoming to outgoing to crossing birds, in various combinations. There were bounding rabbits and springing teal, and each station was given a fanciful name and natural features like ponds, thickets, and heavily wooded shooting alleys were employed to add realism. A day at sporting clays was like a nature walk with a shotgun.

Alison Caselman shooting clays from the high tower.

As well as the standard trap or skeet clay pigeon, clay targets were developed in new sizes and shapes. There were smaller, faster ones, mid-sized standard clays, and ultra-hard disc-shaped clays to bound along the ground like rabbits. Some are thrown upside-down to give a looping arc.

It was not long before the American mania for standardization, score keeping, and national rankings led to fundamental changes in the game of sporting clays, something that guided it, at least in part, down the same path skeet had trodden 75 years earlier. Every skeet range, by regulation, is exactly the same as every other, making national rankings possible. Sporting clays ranges, however, are like golf courses. Some are more difficult than others.

The first major change to sporting clays was to allow shooters to call for the bird with the gun already mounted and the safety off. This simple change set in motion a train of events. Suddenly, some targets were too easy. So, they were made more difficult, and this, in turn, led to the development of harder-hitting, faster loads. These firecrackers required heavier guns to tame the recoil, while birds thrown at greater distances demanded longer barrels. Pretty soon, the average "sporting gun" was as elaborately specialized as any trap gun, complete with 34-inch ported barrels, Monte Carlo stocks, an array of interchangeable choke tubes you'd need a computer to keep track of, and golf carts to carry it all between the stations. The sporting clays shooter who still wanted to use his hunting gun and get in some fun and practice in the off-season suddenly found himself faced with targets that bore no resemblance to any shot you would see in the field, and ones you'd never dream of shooting at if you did. Sporting clays became a game for

the obsessively competitive, complete with scorecards, lifetime records, and national rankings, just like trap and skeet. Now, at many shooting clubs today, you find different sporting clays courses, ranked by difficulty of targets, which allow the average hunter with a pump gun to get in some realistic practice, while across the way the dedicated sporting shooters with their $10,000 over/unders can compete against each other to their hearts' content.

One benefit of all this, aside from enriching the shotgun and ammunition makers, has been a proliferation of imaginative shooting stations and presentations. High towers that throw clays from 30 yards up and everything in between are now to be found in every state, and some of them rival the towers used to simulate high pheasants in England. This makes top-level shotgun practice widely available where it never was before.

As for guns, shotgun makers have been frantically producing dedicated sporting guns. Almost all are over/unders, with a scattering of semi-autos and pumps. Someone wanting to shoot all the competition disciplines can buy a gun like the Blaser F3 and get interchangeable buttstocks and fore-ends and a wide variety of barrels in every gauge, and use one gun for everything, merely changing the configuration according to what they want to shoot that day. A state-of-the-art sporting gun with 34-inch barrels can change into an international trap gun, from there into a .410 skeet gun, and from there to a game gun to shoot quail over dogs, using nothing but a hex wrench.

AND ALL THE OTHERS ...

The games just described are the most widely practiced of the shotgun sports, but

Alison and Prairie Grove owner Ralph Gates.

there are several others, with new ones appearing, it seems, all the time.

Cowboy Action is easily the most colorful. Competitors dress in Old West clothing, give themselves names like "Rattlesnake Rick," and shoot blackpowder revolvers, lever-action rifles, and hammer shotguns. Everything possible is done to make the competitions realistic, from the configuration of the guns involved to the loads allowed. Cowboy Action enthusiasts can become as deeply involved as Civil War re-enactors, in getting every period detail exactly right. The shotgun side, shot mostly with reproduction hammer guns, involves blackpowder, buckshot, and stationary targets. The gunfight at the OK Corral, in which Doc Holliday is believed to have used a double-barrel 10-gauge hammer gun, is a favorite theme.

At the other end of the scale, in gentility, if not moderation, are the Vintagers, formally known as the Order of Edwardian Gunners. These are enthusiasts of the English shotgun, the great driven shoots at Sandringham and Holkham, and the exploits of Lords Ripon and Walsingham. Participants dress in Edwardian suits and gowns and use vintage Lancasters, Woodwards, and Purdeys, with and without hammers, in a variety of competitions using clay targets. The proceedings usually include an Edwardian lunch or evening gala.

Devotees of the black guns have their own modern discipline, 3-Gun shooting. Like Cowboy Action, 3-Gun uses handguns, rifles, and shotguns. These firearms, however, are ultra-modern. A dedicated 3-Gun shotgun will have an extended magazine, collapsible stock,

Ryan Mason and Alison Caselman shooting doubles off the high tower.

The high tower also has a shooting platform for shooting out-going birds at all heights.

red-dot sights, and flashlight under the muzzle. The shooting simulates combat or self-defense situations. While the Vintagers shoot at clays in the air, shotgun targets with both Cowboy Action and 3-Gun are more likely to be stationary, representing bad guys shooting back at you, rather than driven grouse in flight.

On the live game side of things, there is a worldwide pig scourge, with feral hogs of all kinds, from domestic pigs gone wild to genuine wild boar and various crossbreeds in between, overrunning plantations and farm fields from Texas to Germany. Shooting driven wild boar has been a staple of European hunting for centuries. In America, hunting the many hogs that are devastating agriculture and destroying other species is becoming both a hunting activity and an exercise in survival.

While most hog hunting is done with rifles, driven boar can be taken with shotguns loaded with buckshot, and some shooting clubs have created simulated driven boar games, with the role of the pigs played by everything from trash-can lids to five-gallon buckets and, in one immortal instance, pumpkins. Buckshot is the preferred ammunition but, depending on the range, birdshot also works well.

The tactical shotgun in competition use. This is Brittany Workman, of the Top Gun indoor shooting range, in Missouri, shooting bowling pins with a Benelli. While this gun is outfitted for 3-Gun competition, it is an equally good working tactical gun for home- and self-defense.

CHAPTER 9

SHOTGUNS FOR GAME

A Beretta 20-gauge over/under, an excellent gun for bobwhite quail such as these, in Mexico.

Since the late 1700s in France, the art of "shooting-flying" has centered on shooting game birds on the wing. All modern shotguns are descended from game guns, and most modern shooting games were originated to simulate game shooting of some kind.

Just as competition guns have become highly specialized, unsuited to any purpose other than that for which they were designed, we have also come around to at least an informal specialization in game guns. The ideal dove gun of today is hardly suited to hunting geese, and a gun you would take into the woods for woodcock is not what you would choose for wild pheasants in the Dakotas. This is not to say that one gun cannot be made to do everything, because it certainly can. Whether it will do everything *well* is another question.

UPLAND GAME

Before diving into the specifics of what gun for what bird, the author has a pet theory he would like to share with you, based on an experience in South Africa, in 1994. I arrived there with an old Joseph Lang 12-bore with 27-inch barrels choked IC/M. In the run-up to the election, with the African National

An E.M. Reilly 12-bore, made around 1890, a lovely quail gun with one-ounce loads.

This is a Grulla Armas double gun, made specifically for hunting ruffed grouse and woodcock.

Congress expected to win and everyone very nervous, ammunition was in extremely short supply. All we could find for six weeks of mixed-bag wingshooting were a few cases of skeet loads shooting one ounce of No. 9 shot.

On the list of huntable species were everything from tiny button quail (about the size of a shotshell) to spur-winged geese, which resemble a B-17. In between, there were francolin, guinea fowl, grey partridge and, every afternoon, flights of doves. We also spent several afternoons waist-deep in swamp water, prowling through the reeds, shooting ducks, coots, and geese.

Having no choice as to gun, choke, or load, I shot what I had and made allowances. After six weeks, I wasn't missing all that much, and nothing I hit was getting away. You get to the point where you know exactly what the gun is capable of and you

Driven pheasants in Idaho, shooting a Pedro Arrizabalaga double, and an H.J. Hussey.

make it happen, subconsciously calculating which barrel to use.

This experience gave rise to a completely unprovable theory, but one I firmly believe to be true: If a hunter went through life with only one gun, choked only one way, and simply learned to use it and adapt to situations, at the end of 50 years he would have bagged more birds than the man with many guns who constantly switches around and changes chokes and loads. The man with one gun learns to know that gun and its capabilities like the back of his hand.

This is not an argument that endears you to gun makers, but it provides lively conversation when you get tired of the hunting videos.

The major limiting factor in game gun performance today is the requirement for non-lead shot on some game birds. These restrictions also apply to upland game in some situations, such as hunting pheasants on state preserves in South Dakota. By and large, however, the upland game gun remains much what it was a hundred years ago. What worked then will work today.

The Pheasant Gun

Pheasants in America today are hunted in two ways: There are the wild pheasants of the Dakotas and Midwest, and there are released birds, hunted on shooting estates and preserves all over the country. Almost all are walked up with pointing dogs, but some estates stage driven shoots, in which released birds are driven to waiting guns by a line of beaters.

Let's begin by looking at what kind of gun will do the job. If I were to go to South Dakota tomorrow to hunt wild pheasants, I would take a 12 gauge with 28- to 30-inch barrels, choked IC/M or something similarly open, with one-ounce loads of No. 7½ shot. Although many modern authorities and most outfitters insist you need heavy loads, even 3-inch magnums loaded with big shot at high velocities, this has not been my experience at all. As well, if you shoot that kind of ammunition, you will need a gun eight or nine pounds to dampen the recoil, and such a heavy gun is hard to handle, especially after you've been carrying it all day. The rationale for these outfitters' advice is that wild pheasants flush at long ranges—60 to 80 yards, according to some—and you need to be able to shoot them way out there or not get your limit.

In both North and South Dakota, the daily limit is three cock birds. While many birds do flush a long way out, especially late in the season, after they've been chased for a few months, it is by no means absolute, and I have never hunted the Dakotas where I did not get more than enough chances to

A Pedro Arrizabalaga 12-bore, with Maggie and a dead pheasant, in Idaho.

shoot three roosters at reasonable ranges. Those days when I have collected only one or none, there were generally no birds in the vicinity, either near or far.

In 1913, Sir Ralph Payne-Gallwey published a book called *High Pheasants in Theory and Practice*, a slim volume that is still in print and should be read by every pheasant hunter. Sir Ralph was an aristocrat of independent means and a dedicated shooter with an inquiring turn of mind. An accomplished amateur scientist so typical of the late Victorian era, he conducted a series of experiments regarding killing power, penetration, and shot size. His conclusion, based on his own extensive testing and experiments, was that smaller shot like No. 6 (our No. 7) kills pheasants better than larger shot like No. 4 (our No. 5). More pellets mean you are more likely to hit the head and kill instantly, and also get multiple hits on the body.

Interestingly, a testimonial appears in a catalog of one smaller ammunition company that markets a heavy 12-gauge shell, loaded with 1¼ ounces (or more, if you want it), of No. 7½ shot. It seems the writer ran out of this load while in the Dakotas and turned to a high-brass, heavy load of No. 4s. Immediately, he began experiencing wounding, running birds, lost birds. While I don't see the need for quite so much of it, I would go so far as to say that any hunter, using any gun in any gauge, is better off with No. 7½ for pheasants than any other shot size.

Elsewhere, I have mentioned a pheasant hunt in North Dakota, where we hunted in 60 mile per hour winds. The birds flushed far and rode that wind like Valkyries, yet we had no trouble killing them with B&P High Pheasant loads in No. 7 shot, in both 12- and 20-gauge, either one ounce or, in the 20s, ⅞-ounce. The trick is to hit the birds, not belt yourself into the next county.

Unlike big game, killing birds reliably is not dependent on one or more pellets penetrating to the vitals. Instead, pellets

The author hunting quail, in Alabama, with a Charles Lancaster 12-bore.
Photo by J. Guthrie

stun, break wings, and cause the bird to fall from the air. If it falls from high enough, the impact of hitting the ground will either stun or kill it.

To give another real-life example of the power of multiple pellet hits, in 1998, I was accidentally shot, hit by five No. 7 pellets from a distance of about 125 yards. All five hit me in the face. I instantly dropped to my knees, just from the impact. All five pellets drew blood, but none penetrated. At 125 yards, those pellets did not have much

Wild quail in the Georgia pines. The hunter is using a 20-gauge double.

energy left, but they had enough for serious shock effect. So, imagine the effect on a hard-flying pheasant at 30 yards, when the pellets are moving fast.

Although most hunters use a 12-gauge gun, there is no reason not to hunt pheasants with any gauge you choose. If you prefer a small gauge, then you should choke it tightly to get a denser pattern, shoot carefully, and limit your shots to closer ranges.

In a 12-gauge, Improved Cylinder is the most useful of all chokes for pheasant hunting, but a good case can be made for Modified, which, in most guns, gives the best pattern over the widest range of distances. Full choke is the least useful, unless you plan to take only long shots; a hunter with a single-barrel gun and Full choke is limiting his chances severely. In a 20-gauge, I would go with Modified and, for a 28, it's Full choke, shorter ranges, and shoot for the head.

The Quail Gun

As with the pheasant, there are two types of bobwhite quail in America: wild and pen-raised. There are also other species of quail, including Mearns', Gambel's, valley quail, and so on. All of these species other than bobwhites are wild birds and present most of the same challenges as the wild bobwhite.

To give an idea of how approaches can vary, regarding the ideal bobwhite quail gun, consider this: I know of one ranch in Texas, where they hunt only wild quail, that will not allow the use of any gun *larger* than 20-gauge. There is also a plantation in Georgia, devoted to the raising and shooting of wild bobwhites, that will not allow the use of any gun *smaller* than 20-gauge.

In the first case, the rationale is that they want guests (there is limited commercial hunting), to shoot smaller guns with tighter chokes and make either clean kills or clean misses. In the second case, there is no commercial hunting, and the owners want their guests to avoid wounding birds, by carrying open-choked guns with sufficient pellets to get clean kills.

And right there, boiled down, you have the debate over quail guns that has bubbled on for a century.

We can assume that just about anything can be used effectively on pen-raised birds that flush from close in and do not fly with the same vigor as their wild brethren. But what do you need for a wild bobwhite?

The ideal quail gun shoots from ¾- to a full ounce of shot, No. 7½ to No. 9, from a relatively open choke. It weighs closer to six pounds than seven and has barrels long enough to give a smooth, sustained swing. That description fits any number of guns in 12-, 16-, or 20-gauge, and even a few 28s. When you get down to .410, if your host allows it, you will have less shot and need a tighter choke to get a lethal killing pattern at any range over about 20 yards. Then again, even wild quail are not shot at much over 30 yards. They either hold for the dog and flush close and hard, or they run and don't flush at all. Rarely do they run and then flush at 40 or 50 yards. For a good day

of quail shooting, the trick is not so much to hit the birds that are far out, as it is not to miss the ones that are close in.

As for gun types, any will do as long as you can handle it fast and shoot it straight. Some of the best bobwhite hunters of the ages swore by a 16- or 20-gauge pump, such as a Winchester Model 12 or Remington 31. Today, some fanatical bobwhite hunters use Model 42 pump-action .410s, but they are a highly skilled minority.

In a modern gun, a good 20-gauge over/under or semi-auto, with 28- or 30-inch barrels, using 2¾-inch shotshells with ⅞- or an ounce of shot, is just about perfect. If you can find a light 12-gauge weighing 6¼ to 6¾

Typical ruffed grouse country demands a gun that comes up quickly, but will sustain a swing. That is more important than mere light weight.

pounds and shoot one-ounce loads of No. 8s, you should get patterns close to perfect and a gun that handles quickly and effectively.

The Dove Gun

The 28-gauge is usually touted as everyone's dream dove gun, because it is fast handling for close-in, swooping, diving, and jinking birds. This is all very well for about five percent of the wingshooters out there. For the rest of us, such a light, whippy gun will lead to more misses than hits.

Doves coming in to decoys resemble ducks doing the same thing and, for these

birds, a 28 is just fine—but then, pretty much anything will work. If you are farther along the flyway, where doves are coming overhead on their way somewhere, a long-barreled 12 shooting one or $1^{1}/_{8}$ ounces of shot in No. $7\frac{1}{2}$ or No. 8 through a Modified choke, gives a good pattern for distant birds. Here, the key is not so much a fast poke as a smooth swing, getting well out ahead of the bird and putting your shot cloud where it belongs.

On one of the best days I ever had on doves, I was using a 12-gauge pigeon gun, made in England, in 1904, with tulip chokes that, by modern measurement, would be called Light Modified and Modified. Its patterns are even and consistent. For ammunition, I used B&P Competition One, with $^{7}/_{8}$-ounce of No. 8s.

Most commonly, what you see in the dove fields are 20-gauge semi-autos, whether Benelli, Beretta, or Browning, and these work beautifully in the right hands. They are the standard guns for the high-volume dove shooting of Argentina and other parts

A Charles Lancaster 12-gauge double with a spruce grouse.

of South America, and work just as well over sunflowers in Louisiana.

The Grouse & Woodcock Gun

Here, we can combine guns for both ruffed grouse and woodcock, which are hunted in much the same way and under the same conditions. Usually, the prescription is for a short-barreled, light gun that will not get hung up in brush, one that you can carry all day and shoot quickly. Generally, the nostalgists will plump for a 16-gauge, preferably a Parker or Fox, while the modern realists insist on a 12-gauge semi-auto that is almost a tactical gun.

Since even diehard grouse hunters can't agree on the ideal gun, recommending one or the other is fraught with risk. However, consider this: Most authorities say you will carry the gun more than shoot it, which is certainly true. Still, when the time comes for one of those rare shots, do you want to hit the bird or not? Choosing a gun because it's easy to carry seems to be reversing

one's priorities. Better to carry a heavier gun, walk less, and hunt smarter, if that's what it takes to down a bird or two.

For my part, I prefer a light 12-gauge with barrels 28 to 30 inches long, for a smooth swing. Much of the time, with grouse, you will be swinging on a bird you can barely see, shooting largely from instinct. Best to have a gun that will carry on regardless, rather than one that will stop swinging the moment you lose eye contact.

Although an ounce of shot is more than enough for the light-boned, somewhat fragile ruffed grouse, it may not be enough when you take into account the brush, leaves, and pine needles that may absorb a good portion of the shot charge before it reaches the bird. For this reason, I like Federal's Extra-Lite trap loads for grouse, $1\frac{1}{8}$ ounces of No. $7\frac{1}{2}$ shot at 1,100 fps. It is soft shooting in the lightest 12-gauge, but very effective.

For North America's other grouse—the sharptail of the west, the spruce grouse of

Side-lever Boss & Co. 12-bore with ruffed grouse. This gun has 30-inch barrels – not generally recommended for grouse, but it is light over all (6½ pounds) and the barrels sustain the swing.

Duck hunting in South Dakota can require a specialized shotgun.

A Ruger Red Label 12-gauge.

the north—any gun that works on either ruffed grouse or pheasant is more than adequate, and the same applies to the Hungarian partridge and chukar. For the chukar, an additional consideration is terrain and, thus, what kind of gun you want to carry up and down mountainsides.

WATERFOWL

Because waterfowl are migratory birds, federal regulations require they be hunted with non-lead shot. This is commonly referred to as "non-toxic," and while that definition is open to argument, it has become standard terminology.

Non-toxic shot is anything that does not contain lead. The most common alternative is steel, which is really iron. Iron is not as heavy as lead, and it is considerably harder. Where a column of lead shot will compress readily as it passes through a tight choke, steel will not. Nor will pure tungsten, which, while heavier than lead, is harder

than steel, as well as very expensive. For these reasons, guns have been developed that will shoot steel effectively, without suffering any harm from either abraded barrels or damaged chokes.

When you combine these realities with the fact that almost all good waterfowl hunting is done in bad weather, around mud and water and salt spray, the use of "fine" guns for waterfowling is almost a thing of the past. Although you can get legal non-toxic loads that are usable in old double guns, the combination of difficulty, expense, and inconvenience generally means that hunting ducks with your Dad's old L.C. Smith is a once-a-year stroll down memory lane, not a regular practice.

Another consideration is the need for camouflage. Modern duck hunters go out clad head to toe in camouflage clothing, complete with facemasks, as well as every item of equipment patterned in either RealTree or Mossy Oak. The shotgun is no exception. A nice old double can be

Doves in Argentina. There are more than a hundred doves in this photograph, taken at random near a sunflower field. This is high-volume shooting.

wrapped in camouflage tape to hide its outlines and dull its gleam, but most of us would rather not do that. These reasons, combined with the fact that you can buy a perfectly good, factory-camouflaged, steel-shot-safe and practically indestructible pump gun for a few hundred bucks, means that most hunters have a dedicated waterfowl gun. Another advantage is that, with interchangeable choke tubes, your camouflaged beauty can also serve as your turkey gun.

The Duck Gun

The limitations of non-toxic shot dictate that the standard duck gun today is a 12-gauge, with a few fanatics using 10-gauge guns. Tens have staged a modest comeback in recent years, purely because of the need for non-toxic shot. The limitations of steel require larger pellets to procure the same effectiveness downrange, which means larger charges to get the same number of pellets in the pattern, which means

The late writer James Guthrie, in North Dakota, with a wild pheasant and his custom 20-bore AYA on a day when the winds were 60 miles per hour.

The retrieve after the shot on a driven pheasant shoot, in England. Note the gun safely broken over the shooter's right arm.

larger cartridges to hold the larger charges and the commensurate increase in powder.

The 3½-inch 12-gauge was developed for exactly this purpose, but a 10-gauge gun can also accommodate these loads comfortably. The extra weight of a 10-gauge gun dampens the recoil nicely, and a 10-gauge will generally deliver better patterns with heavy charges of shot than will a long 12.

For an all-around duck gun, you can hardly do better than a pump or semi-auto. Both are durable and, with a 28- or even 26-inch barrel, have sufficient length for a smooth swing. If you intend to do a lot of pass shooting for ducks, as opposed to calling them in to decoys, you might want to go to a longer barrel.

The key to a variety of duck-hunting situations is to have a selection of choke tubes. For ducks over decoys, open chokes, for long-range pass shooting, tighter chokes. In either instance, one must be careful to use choke tubes specifically rated for use with steel shot.

As for the loads themselves, although the modern trend is for heavy loads of big pellets at high velocities, a skilled hunter can do very well with conventional 2¾-inch 12-gauge loads, with smaller pellets (No. 6 instead of No. 4). As with pheasants, more and smaller pellets mean a denser pattern and a better chance of a head shot, especially over decoys. At longer ranges, however, larger pellets are preferable for their ability to retain velocity and killing power.

The Goose Gun

At one time in America, there was almost a separate category of shotguns called "goose guns." A typical example was the old Marlin bolt-action shotgun with a 36-inch barrel choked Full. This was intended for high pass shooting at geese and, apparently, the notion sold well enough that the gun stayed in production for years.

Today, more geese are decoyed into grain fields and ambushed from camouflaged hides than in any other way. This is

Three faces of the Benelli semi-auto.

Two quite different Benelli game guns.

Benelli's Super Vinci waterfowl gun.

an exciting way to hunt, but, for this kind of shooting, your gun should resemble a short-barreled tactical gun more than the traditional long Tom. Rising from a hide to surprise a flock coming in demands a gun that is compact and easy to handle. Ranges are generally not long—similar to decoyed ducks, or even less—and deliberate head shots with a cloud of pellets is not only possible, but recommended.

Geese and their even larger relations, the swans and cranes, are big birds whose bodies can carry off a lot of shot. Getting even the minimum penetration is difficult. So, as with ducks, there are loads for decoyed geese and loads for pass shooting. If the 3½-inch 12-gauge has any real place, this is it, and a 10-gauge is even better. The

10-gauge is to the magnum 12 what the 12 is to the magnum 20: While the paper ballistics may be similar, pattern quality and overall shooting performance is superior.

THE TURKEY GUN

Turkeys are a category unto themselves, because turkey hunting, as it is practiced today, is unlike any other kind of bird shooting with a shotgun. Turkeys are most often called in to decoys, they are shot on the ground, ideally when they are motionless, and the target is the turkey's neck. A turkey neck is about two inches in diameter, and typical ranges run 15 to 40 yards. To place a killing number of pellets in the neck and head at longer yardages, you need a

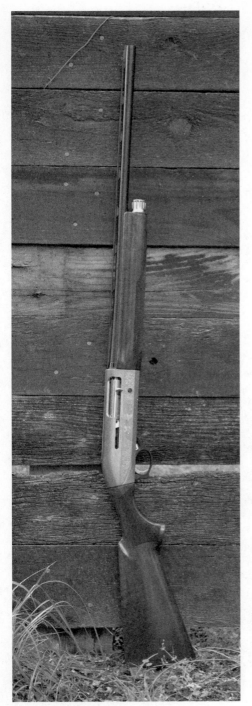

The Benelli Duca di Montefeltro 20-bore, a more traditional upland gun.

Full choke. Although many turkey guns have long barrels, they are not necessary for ballistic performance; the pattern size is determined by the choke tube. So, any pump or semi-auto with a 26-inch barrel will be fine for turkeys.

Fortunately, lead shot is still allowed for turkeys, so the turkey gun is not a complicated concept. Almost any 12-gauge will do just fine. One absolute requirement is camouflage, and any turkey hunter who goes out without camouflaging everything, gun included, is severely handicapping himself. Finally, though all the manufacturers offer dedicated turkey guns with camouflage tailored to specific situations, a duck or goose gun can easily be adapted to turkey hunting.

One important consideration in choosing your turkey gun is noise. When stalking and calling turkeys, any kind extraneous noise must be kept to an absolute minimum from the moment you leave your vehicle, and the clang of a semi-auto slamming shut easily carries half a mile on a still morning. A pump is only marginally better. For this reason, and because of the element of possible surprise, turkey guns are carried with a round in the chamber and the safety on. Of course, having a loaded gun, crawling through thickets and swamps and negotiating rough terrain that only a grouse hunter would attempt, raises issues of safe gun handling that every turkey hunter should keep in mind. Hunting by one's self, it is easy to forget about this.

GUNS FOR DEER AND BIG GAME

More and more states are mandating shotgun-only seasons for whitetails. Shotguns are also used for hunting black bears and mountain lions.

Although a standard shotgun can be used with slugs or buckshot, the hunter is at a severe disadvantage using one. The modern big-game shotgun has a rifled barrel, rifle sights, and shoots sabot slugs that are effective out to 200 yards; this is a far cry from the deer gun of the 1960s, where 75 yards was a long, long way.

The big problem with slugs is not so much their downrange effectiveness as it is putting a cumbersome slug on target. Sights solve this problem to a great degree. The old Foster slug, which resembled a Minié ball with raised fins to (theoretically) impart some spin, was a small step up from the old round lead ball—the "pumpkin ball"—but not a great deal. A sabot slug, where a proper bullet is enclosed in a nylon jacket that grips rifling, then falls away as the bullet exits the muzzle, turns the shotgun into a good, mid-range hunting gun.

Although some hunters still use buckshot, its use is becoming rarer, with buckshot today usually reserved for tactical use. Those who hunt with buckshot should pattern their gun

Alison with a 28-gauge Ruger Red Label. The Red Label introduced the over/under to a generation of Americans, at an affordable price.

Alison with a Benelli semi-auto 12-gauge.

with their chosen load to see exactly what it is doing at what distances. Most people are surprised at just how quickly a buckshot pattern deteriorates into ragged nothingness.

Today's deer hunting shotgun comes in any number of shapes. There are pumps and semi-autos with short barrels, rifle sights, and rifled bores. These can double as utility guns for the pickup or as home-defense weapons. They are inexpensive and extremely durable.

In the 1890s, Holland & Holland perfected a design called the Paradox, a conventional side-by-side double shotgun that had a six-inch length of rifling near the muzzle. Invented by Lt. Col. George Vincent Fosbery, VC, the Paradox was a popular and effective all-around gun for use in India and Africa. Holland & Holland loaded special Paradox ammunition with a solid lead slug of its own design. This was a hard-hitting combination, effective even on lions and tigers out beyond a hundred yards.

Other London gun makers followed with variations on the theme. Today, these guns in good condition sell for thousands of dollars, so the opportunity to pick one up for local whitetail hunting is limited at best. The point is,

though, that a good side-by-side double offers the same advantages to the big-game hunter as a double rifle: extremely silent operation and with two very fast shots packing a real punch.

Tony Galazan offers a slug gun version of his RBL boxlock shotgun called the Professional. It has 24-inch barrels, a pistol grip, a broad fore-end, and rifle sights. It is grooved to accept scope rings. There is a movable collet connecting the barrels at the muzzle. The gun is sighted in with the left barrel aligned to the scope; the collet is then adjusted to bring the right barrel into alignment and, just like that, you have two barrels shooting to the same point of impact, like a good double rifle. It is available only in 20-gauge, but, with today's sabot slugs, a 20-gauge is an excellent deer gun at normal deer-hunting ranges. These guns also serve well for coyotes, feral hogs, and other varmints that are shot with buckshot at close ranges.

A Mossberg 500 in slug gun guise costs a few hundred dollars, where the Galazan Professional will run you about $5,000, which just goes to prove that, no matter what your shotgun activity, there is something for every taste and bank account.

Ryan with the Benelli Super Vinci.

CHAPTER 10

THE TACTICAL SHOTGUN

The shotgun used for tactical purposes—military, police, and self-defense—is, in most ways, completely different than a sporting or competition gun. Modern tactical guns have black composite stocks, short barrels, and sights like a rifle. Some have folding metal stocks, while others have no buttstock at all, just a pistol grip. They are designed to shoot either buckshot or slugs and be used at close range. Today, almost all are either semi-automatic or pump guns, although, for centuries, the short-barreled side-by-side double was the dominant design.

The tradition of using shotguns for self-defense goes back a long way. Even designing shotguns for that express purpose isn't new. The blunderbuss was the first "tactical" shotgun, used on naval vessels either to repel boarders or quell mutinies, and on land by stagecoach drivers, to guard against highwaymen. The bell-shaped shotgun muzzle, so beloved by cartoonists, began with the blunderbuss—which actually had such a muzzle, if not quite so pronounced.

The most famous use of a tactical shotgun was by John Henry "Doc" Holliday at the OK Corral, in Tombstone, Arizona, in 1881. To this day, there is no absolutely reliable account as to what the gun was

An early "tactical" shotgun, an E.M. Reilly hammer gun, dating from the 1870s, that revels in shooting both buckshot and ball.

or who owned it. It has been variously reported as a 12-bore Colt Lightning, a 10-bore W.W. Greener, and various others. Historians believe, however, that the gun was the Greener. It is known that Virgil Earp visited the Wells Fargo office that morning and borrowed one of its shotguns. Wells Fargo used Greeners in both 10- and 12-bore, generally giving 12s to their security guards and reserving the larger guns for stagecoach duty. As the confrontation loomed, Earp handed the gun over to Holliday.

The typical gun of a stagecoach guard was a large-bore side-by-side hammer gun with short barrels, usually loaded with buckshot. From this, the term "riding shotgun" found its way into the everyday lexicon of American life. On a stagecoach, the shotgun was the ideal weapon; any dispute was likely to be at short range, and there is nothing quite so intimidating as looking down the muzzle of a 12-bore. The 12-bore "coach gun" lives on, in the form of reproduction shotguns and shotgun events in Cowboy Action shooting. Oh, and by the way, the second-most famous such shotgun, this one fictional, was in the hands of Steve McQueen, as he rode shotgun on a hearse in the opening scenes of *The Magnificent Seven*.

A more formal use of the tactical shotgun was the "trench gun" of the Great War. When America joined the fray, in 1917, among the weapons the soldiers carried to France were 12-gauge shotguns with short barrels, often fitted with sling swivels and bayonet lugs. The Winchester '97 pump was the quintessential trench gun—durable, reliable, and deadly, holding a half-dozen rounds of buckshot in its tubular magazine. For a weapon used in hand-to-hand fighting in a trench, it would be difficult to come up with a better choice. Ever since, American pump gun designs have been produced in either a trench gun or tactical configuration.

Since 1918, the tactical shotgun has been more the province of the police than the military. With the buttstock cut off behind the pistol grip, an 18- or 20-inch barrel, and in stainless steel with composite grips, it is carried in the backs of police cars, in the windows of pickup trucks, as survival weapons by bush pilots, and by prospectors in grizzly country.

Some tactical shotgun designs have been fanciful. The SPAS-12, a Franchi creation made immortal by Arnold Schwarzenegger in *The Terminator,* combines both pump- and semi-auto technology to give the user whichever he wants, whenever he needs it. Unfortunately, the SPAS-12 requires someone with arms like Schwarzenegger to handle it, since it weighs 10½ pounds fully loaded. Because of the way it was portrayed in that movie 30 years ago, the SPAS-12 has been on every politician's wish-list of guns to be banned, though, in reality, it is no more threatening than a skeet gun.

Another shotgun that makes the list is the "Street Sweeper," a 12-gauge with a 12-inch barrel, and a 12-round drum magazine that employs the revolver principle. Exactly how practical it is for any purpose whatsoever is debatable, but it certainly looks threatening, and it seems to make everyone's list of "fun guns," as well as every list of guns to be banned.

On the author's gun rack is a 20-bore hammer gun made by E.M. Reilly, in London, in 1874. It actually began life as a .577 Snider double rifle and was later bored out and converted to a shotgun, probably because of corrosion or, perhaps, a shortage of .577 ammunition. At this stage, it is impossible to tell. With 24-inch barrels, the gun weighs a little over seven pounds. It is intriguing to reflect on where it's been and what it might have done in the intervening 140 years.

Learning the basics of shooting a tactical gun.

That aside, it is an endearing little thug. Loaded with blackpowder and a 20-gauge lead ball weighing 350 grains and launched at 850 fps, it is a fearsome little weapon at close range, considerably more powerful than a .45 Auto, and no one has ever accused the .45 of lacking stopping power. If I was a sailor considering mutiny and the first mate walked out on deck with this gun in his hands, I would think again.

One of the most potent features a tactical gun has going for it is the fact that it *looks* frightening. This is not important with a grizzly bear, but it certainly is with a mutinous crew or a lynch mob outside the jail. Just knowing the guards will be armed with sawed-off shotguns is a serious deterrent to a train robber. For a citizen looking for a gun for home-defense, one of the modern, short, tactical guns is more practical (and, ultimately, a lot safer for all concerned), than either a powerful handgun or a semi-automatic rifle of the AR class.

As well, it doesn't matter who happens to be holding the 12-gauge at the time. Home invaders, confronted by a 12-year old kid or a tiny woman behind the yawning muzzle of a shotgun, are more likely to back off than if they find themselves facing the same person with a pistol. It doesn't take a lot of thought to see why: Subconsciously, we know that, with a sawed off shotgun, skill with the weapon is not as critical as it is with a pistol or a rifle. This question of skill may or may not be true, in fact, but that's not the point. What counts is our immediate reaction, and, when you see a person wielding a shotgun, the immediate reaction is to back off.

* * *

The original coach and trench guns were very basic. Not so the modern tactical gun. Partly because of the march of technology and partly because of the demands of competition, tactical shotguns

Among the earliest tactical shotguns were the "trench guns" from the Great War (1914-'18). They had short barrels, sling swivels, and bayonet lugs.

A variety of tactical shotguns, used for both tactical shooting games and serious self-defense.

of course you can, if you have the right ammunition. However, a gun with a military-style pistol grip and iron sights does not lend itself to a conventional mount and swing. And, with their generally shorter stocks, they are intended to be shot tactical-style, like an AR-15 or other military rifle.

Today, every major manufacturer of either pump or semi-auto shotguns produces a tactical model. While most are 12-gauge, 20-gauge tactical guns are also available. In both, the 3-inch chamber is standard, logical for using buckshot and slugs in both gauges.

For the non-competitor interested in a gun for home-defense purposes, the tactical shotgun is an imminently practical choice. They are rugged, reliable, easy to use, intimidating to look at, and deadly when used correctly. At the same time, buckshot is a short-range weapon with minimal penetrative powers, compared to ammunition from most rifles and even handguns. Buckshot isn't likely to perforate a wall and accidentally hurt someone on the other side. In fact, for defensive purposes at close range, any load of birdshot is effective—besides, the bad guy isn't going to know what you have loaded.

The first tactical gun, the blunderbuss, was a single-barrel gun. Next came doubles, then pumps, and now the standard is the semi-auto. However, pump guns still have their place and are preferred by many, because of their simplicity and reliability. Pump guns work well and they keep on working, with the shooter providing the motivating power. They do not clog up with powder residue and jam. A skilled man with a pump gun can put more shots downrange faster than the fastest semi-auto—but, perhaps, this is arguing how many angels can dance on the head of a pin. Still, such venerable tactical guns as the Ithaca Model 37 and

have become as elaborate as the most fitted-out AR-15, with optical and laser sights, mounted flashlights, extended magazines, and Picatinny rails that accommodate myriad gadgets. All have sling swivels and iron sights. Generally, barrels are no more than 24 inches, and buttstocks, where they exist at all, are generally shorter than would be called for on a game gun.

Some tactical shotguns, like the Winchester Defender, have only a pistol grip and no buttstock at all. These are intended for shooting from the hip one hundred per cent of the time. Others, like the SPAS-12, have folding buttstocks similar to those found on paratrooper-style military rifles. These can be shot either way, depending on the situation.

Unlike other shotguns, tactical guns are not intended for use on moving targets. This does not mean you can't shoot a moving target with such a gun, because

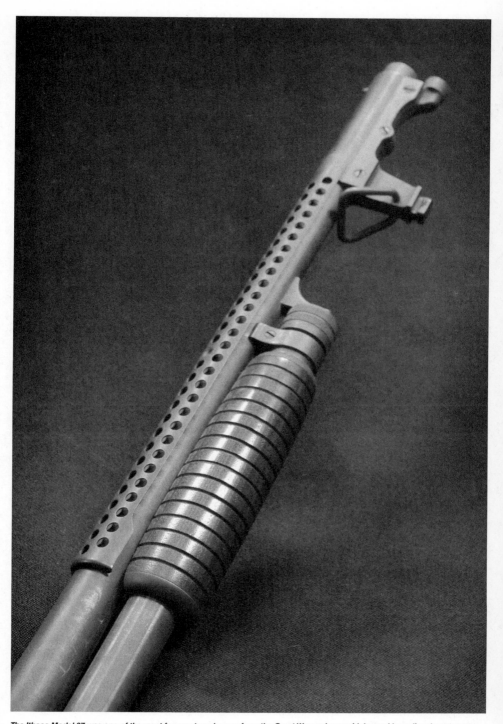

The Ithaca Model 37 was one of the most famous trench guns from the Great War and was widely used by police departments.

Brittany Workman is a shooting instructor who specializes in tactical games. The gun is a Benelli made for the purpose.

Remington 870 pumps are a mainstay of many a police precinct, even if the Beretta and Benelli semi-autos are giving them a run for their money.

Like the AR-15 and Ruger Mini-14 rifles, there is a thriving secondary market in accoutrements for tactical shotguns, such as folding stocks, sights, flashlights, elaborate slings, and any gadget that can be attached to a Picatinny rail. Indeed, if tactical shotguns were formerly plain, inexpensive, low-rent cousins, today's tactical guns for practical shotgun and 3-Gun competitions are quite high-end, costing as much as a refined trap or skeet model. Where, 40 years ago, you would find only two or three dedicated tactical guns in the pages of *Gun Digest*, today there are dozens.

Like the pistol for IPSC competition, so-called tactical shotguns for sporting events have been refined out of all recognition, to the point where some would be of questionable value if called upon for actual tactical work. A modern IPSC .45 Auto, with a long barrel, compensator, special grips, and target sights, held in a holster that is a holster in name only, has little practical use outside the IPSC target ring—ironic, when you consider that "IPSC" stands for "International Practical Shooting Confederation."

Some competitions where shotguns are used, such as Cowboy Action, practical shotgun, and some 3-Gun classes, restrict what may be used. In other events, anything goes, and competitors can trick out their shotguns to look like a circus pony. Cowboy Action, for instance, restricts competitors to shotguns from a particular era, and these are mostly side-by-sides, with some pump guns allowed. They are loaded with blackpowder or blackpowder substitutes.

One area to note, especially if you plan to use a tactical gun for other purposes,

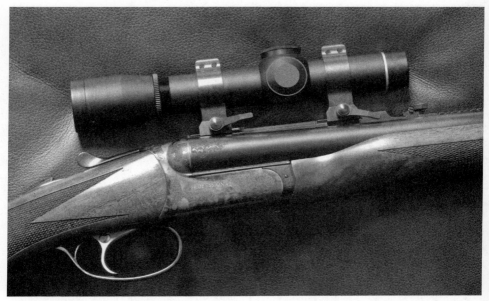

The Professional, a boxlock 20-gauge made for shooting slugs, by Connecticut Shotgun Manufacturing Co. It is set up to shoot more like a double rifle than a shotgun, and the barrel alignment can be adjusted to regulate the gun to shoot different loads to the same point of impact from both barrels.

is magazine capacity. The Street Sweeper holds 12 rounds, the SPAS-12 holds nine, most others hold at least six. Some guns have extended magazines to increase capacity. In hunting with a pump or semi-auto, almost all jurisdictions restrict total firepower to three rounds (one in the chamber and two in the magazine), and the magazine must be plugged to limit capacity to exactly this amount. A tactical shotgun with a longer barrel, choke tubes, composite stock, and weatherproof finish might make a good duck gun for swamp mud and bad weather, but not if the magazine capacity puts you on the wrong side of the law.

***

Anyone acquiring a shotgun for tactical purposes—a truck gun, home-defense, etc.—should spend time, money, and ammunition learning to use it well. This includes loading, unloading, cleaning, and clearing jams, until the operation of the gun in all its facets is subconscious and second nature.

If the gun is kept somewhere in the house, accessible to anyone in the family in the event of an emergency, then everyone should spend a lot of time with the gun, at the range. Simply showing the other members of the family how it is used, where it is kept, and adding "Remember, it's loaded!" is both dangerous and irresponsible.

Certainly, a good way to learn to use the gun is to sign up for some training courses and then embark on a career competing in 3-Gun or Cowboy Action, but not everyone either wants to do this or has the opportunity. As well, there are a couple problems with this approach.

One are the limits imposed by the games themselves. In Cowboy Action, for example, you need a period-correct gun, so, if your home-defense gun is a Model 870 pump, this doesn't help much.

The other limitation is psychological. These games always have dedicated shooters who think of little else, who trick out their guns with every imaginable device, and live or die by their weekly scores. Such enthusiasts can be intimidating to newcomers. This is encountered in every shooting discipline, not just the shotgun sports, but, wherever it is, it can be very discouraging to people who just want a little practice without intense (and artificial) competition. There is no easy way to deal with it, especially if you are going down to the range intent on introducing your spouse, children, or significant other to the use of the shotgun, as well as to get in a little practice yourself. Plainly said, in tactical shotgun use, there are many more aspects to consider than simply how many targets you broke or how many bowling pins you knocked over in how many seconds.

Use of a shotgun for self-defense requires knowledge and practice of loading and unloading, of clearing jams and dealing with unforeseen problems, and doing it quickly and efficiently. You should also practice shooting from the hip as well as the shoulder, and from different gun and body positions. This is not always possible in an atmosphere of competition, no matter how informal such competition might purport itself to be. Although we cover shooting schools and conventional instruction in the next chapter, there are unique aspects to learning to use a tactical gun, so we will deal with those here.

To take an example from the world of handguns, specifically IPSC, the requirements for shooting IPSC in Canada are much more restrictive and formalized than in the United States. In the early '90s, wanting to really learn to handle a revolver, I signed up for an IPSC qualification course in Canada. This involved one full day each week for four weeks, shooting about 500 rounds a day. It culminated in a series of 16 tests of shooting skill, and we had to pass every single one; fail at even one of these tests, and you failed the course, failed to get your badge and, so, were ineligible for any IPSC match. These tests included things like firing two shots, reloading, firing two more, reloading, and firing two more, and those six shots all had to be in a killing zone of the target.

At that time, as now, the standard IPSC gun was a Colt 1911, tricked out like a prom queen, and the standard holster was peculiar to IPSC and useless for anything else. Since my goal was to learn to use my .44, with the intent of carrying it in Alaska, I used a S&W Mountain Gun and a flapped crossdraw hunting holster. Needless to say, I was slower at many of the drills and at a hopeless disadvantage in others, but I persevered, passed all the tests, and even participated in weekly IPSC matches. My goal in those was only that I not finish dead last. This was before the days of separate matches for semi-autos and revolvers. I put up with the comments from the 1911 users and am proud to say that I never once did finish last.

For tactical shotguns, the NRA has a number of courses and certifies instructors to give them. Many local clubs either put on NRA courses or have come up with their own. My handgun club, Top Gun Shooting Sports, in Arnold, Missouri, offers tactical and home-defense shotgun courses, as well as some informal shooting competitions, such as rapid-fire on bowling pins. Top Gun is an indoor range, so such competitions have to be regulated, but it is all conducted in a very informal atmosphere, with the emphasis on simply helping people become better with their shotguns.

Another approach, admittedly more expensive, but a lot of fun, is to go to a shooting academy like Gunsite, near

Sights on the CSMC "Professional" double-barreled slug gun. Note the mechanism for adjusting the regulation of the barrels for different loads.

Prescott, Arizona. Founded by Col. Jeff Cooper many years ago, Gunsite began with pistols, but now offers both rifle and shotgun training for hunting and tactical use. Gunsite's range of courses is listed on its website. For the beginning tactical shotgunner, a course like this is very useful, because it puts you on the right track from the beginning, showing you what you need to practice and how to do so effectively. Over the years, I have been involved in several courses at Gunsite, including heavy and long-range rifle shooting, tactical carbine use, and single-action revolver. My instructor has always been Il Ling New, one of the best of the current tactical instructors in every discipline and a widely experienced hunter, as well.

Il Ling has hunted Cape buffalo with a handgun, successfully and without incident, which is not a claim that many of us can make. She has many repeat clients, hunters and shooters who consider her to be their coach or tutor and who go back for refresher courses on a regular basis. This is an excellent relationship to establish, if you can find an instructor you really like and can communicate with.

Once you have the ground work in place, you need to find a shooting range that has the facilities to allow you to continue your tactical work. Most skeet, trap, or sporting clays ranges do not offer anything like you require, but any good outdoor handgun range probably does, and most of them allow shotguns within certain limits. My other club, the Arnold Pistol & Rifle Club, has ranges for conventional trap and skeet, as well as for 25-, 50-, and 100-yard benchrest rifle ranges, bull's-eye handgun shooting, IPSC, and Cowboy Action, among others. Most important from a tactical shotgun viewpoint are its "combat pits." There are six individual pits, separated by high, thick, concrete walls, each outfitted with a target board and a frame with steel plates. You shoot into a steep hillside and have an earth bank on which you can place clay pigeons or other targets. Shooting at these not only gives a satisfying cloud of dust when you hit, it allows you to see where your shot went if you miss. A combat pit is your own individual range, and you are your own range master, which allows maximum flexibility for practicing what you want to practice, in your own way, at your own pace. For a family learning to use their tactical shotgun, such an arrangement is ideal.

CHAPTER 11

SHOOTING SCHOOLS AND GUN FIT

Shooting instructor Vicki Ash (right) demonstrating a shooting technique to the author.

Everyone learns to shoot in some way. *Learns.* No one is born with the skill, although there is an element of natural talent. Everyone, however, must learn the mechanics of shooting before even the natural ability of the "born shot" can assert itself.

Some buy a gun and a box of shotshells and take it from there, for good or ill, acquiring bad habits along the way. Others are taught by a well-meaning relative. Some read books about shooting and try to

apply the lessons, and others go to a local range and look for an instructor.

Shooting is a skill that requires a certain amount of theoretical knowledge and a great deal of practical application. Often, sitting around a gun club you will hear that "The best teacher is a case of shells!" This has some truth to it—certainly, you would learn from shooting a case of ammunition, which amounts to 250 shots, or about 10 rounds of skeet or trap. If that was all you

The author (shooting) and Vicki Ash, at the Ashes' instruction ground near Houston.

did, however, you would be far more likely to acquire ingrained bad habits than to become a competent shot.

SHOOTING INSTRUCTION

For some reason, Americans especially have the belief that they are "natural" shots, born to carry a gun and hit what they aim at. For years, the very idea of a shooting school was anathema, an insult to their manhood. Yet handling a gun is as much a skill as that of driving a car, and no one questions the value of formal driving instruction before allowing a teenager out on the road at the wheel of a potentially lethal weapon.

Gil Ash and author, at the Ashes' instruction grounds.

This attitude has changed somewhat and, in the United States today, there are many different levels of shooting instruction available. Almost every range has at least one member who offers shooting instruction on a formal or informal basis, and the NRA has a system of classifying and qualifying shooting instructors in every shooting discipline. In this way, the prospective student has at least an idea of the qualifications of the instructor, before paying a dime or firing a shot.

There are also formal shooting schools, where you can enroll for three or four days of concentrated instruction, working with several different instructors. This is an intense and sometimes expensive approach, but, for the beginner, such a school may turn out to be the best investment in the long run. As with any skilled activity, if you start by acquiring basic correct form and, at the same time, dodge bad habits that will be almost impossible to eliminate later, you will be a better shot for life.

The very first step for any shooter seeking instruction is to decide exactly what kind of a shotgunner he or she wants to be. Do you hope to become a pheasant hunter? An informal skeet shooter? An Olympic-class trap shooter? An all-around shooter who dusts clays to keep in form for hunting? A little bit of everything? Or maybe, having not yet done any of these things, you won't know until you try them—in which case, you'd like to start by becoming safe and competent with a shotgun.

These are vital questions, and any instructor who does not ask about your goals as a shotgunner right at the start is not a very good instructor. Chances are, he intends to make you into the kind of shooter *he* is, regardless your preferences.

This chapter will include a good deal of anecdotal experience, the author having enjoyed years of seeing shooting instruction at its best and worst and having met some of the finest shooting instructors in the world, as well as some who may well be good with others, but were far from good with him. I will name names, of both instructors and establishments that offer instruction, but, generally, only if I can recommend them personally. The reason for this is the very first rule for the prospective student: what works for someone else may not work for you at all.

So, back to the first question. What kind of shooter do you want to be? Let's assume the answer is that you want to be a good, all-around shotgunner—safe in the field, a good instinctive shooter who can react to the unexpected, someone who can hold his or her own on a sporting clays range, and one who is at home with flighting doves or flushing pheasants. For this type of shooter, the best possible instruction is what I would call the "English school." English instruction is geared toward game shooting and has been for 150 years. It teaches the student to carry the gun safely, to mount the gun only when the bird appears, and to slip off the safety only as the gun comes to the shoulder. In the English style, the shooter looks relaxed, almost nonchalant. The best English shooters make shotgunning appear effortless.

We can contrast this to an extreme I call the "mid-Missouri skeet stance." This is a style first encountered on a skeet range in Missouri (hence the name), and it was being generally taught to anyone who came to the range looking for instruction. This stance is exaggerated, feet wide apart, crouching like a sumo wrestler, the gun mounted, safety off, and neck, arms, and shoulders rigid. There is no flexibility for reacting to the unexpected, and the swing is as relentless as the pivoting of a naval gun. Workable for American skeet, perhaps, but useless for much else.

The English stance, on the other hand, is loose and relaxed, feet not too close

At the Holland & Holland shooting ground, teaching teenagers proper shooting technique.

At the Holland & Holland shooting grounds near London, instructor Roland Wild works with a teenage shooter on gun mounting.

together, but also not too far apart. The shooter is on the balls of their feet, leaning slightly forward with the weight on the leading foot. The head is slightly forward with the "predator's look" in the eyes, the result of focus and concentration. The body can pivot in any direction—left, right, up, down—responding instantly to whatever target is presented, from a low crossing shot to a screaming incomer. Because the gun is not at the shoulder, the eye has an unobstructed view of whatever comes along, from whatever angle.

The human body has a natural athletic or defensive posture that is used in a wide range of activities: boxing, batting and throwing in baseball, shooting a pistol using the Weaver combat stance, or shooting a rifle offhand. All these employ essentially the same position, and for the same reason: It is the most flexible stance for both offense and defense, allowing you to respond to the unexpected, including an attack. A flushing pheasant, a 95-mile per hour fastball, an incoming clay, or an opponent's left jab all amount to much

the same thing, in athletic terms. At the same time, this is a very relaxed position, with no tense muscles to start shaking. Combined with this relaxed physical stance, the shooter must have laser-like concentration.

FINDING A GOOD INSTRUCTOR

The real purpose of this chapter is not to instruct in shooting, but to show how to find a good instructor. It is important, however, for the prospective student to have some idea of what to look for. An initial few sessions with a bad instructor can be very destructive, not only to your shooting style, but to your outlook and desire to continue shooting.

In 1994, I attended a five-day course of instruction in Vale, Colorado, put on by Holland & Holland. There were 10 instructors and 40 participants. Divided into groups of four, we rotated through one instructor after another. We had two days of shooting, then a day off, followed by the final two days of shooting. It was June, and

Sometimes closing one eye helps eliminate a "master eye" problem. A good instructor can recognize this and help correct it.

it was hot, dry, and draining. The day off in between was most welcome, because you can only take so much intensive instruction before you need a break.

Some of the instructors were from Holland's own shooting grounds outside London, others were freelance English instructors, and about half were Americans. This allowed the extreme range of instructing theories and styles. What I learned most from that course was not so much any shooting style, but rather the fact that I respond well to some instructors but not to others. From some I learned one specific thing well. Others left me confused, and a few even seemed to erase whatever skill I had. Perhaps the most valuable lesson was that the student's personal relationship with an instructor has nothing to do with whether you will learn well from him or her. You can actively dislike your instructor yet gain a great deal, while another person you would cheerfully spend days

with seems unable to impart any meaningful knowledge. Strange, but true.

For example, Dan Carlisle, an American Olympian who has won medals in both trap and skeet and who has a shooting ground in South Carolina, is one of the most intense individuals I have ever met. A very nice guy, but 15 minutes with Dan will turn you into a quivering wreck. What I did learn from him, however, was the value of concentration. And I mean *concentration*! A 45-minute session with Carlisle is draining, to say the least, but, when you finish, you are seeing the printing on the raised edge of the clay as it flies. Another instructor, Keith Lupton, an Englishman transplanted to America, was able to get me shooting to the point where he could tell me which edge of the clay he wanted me to dust, and I could usually do it.

Then there were others, who shall remain nameless only because I no longer remember their names. I gained nothing

In her early 20s, Alison Caselman is a very accomplished competitive shot. She learned proper technique from the beginning, and is now with the University of Missouri shooting team.

and was lucky to be able to hit anything after a session with them. This was where I learned the value of finding the right instructor and then working with that person on a regular basis. Good shooting is not learned in a weekend, nor even over a year or two. It is a lifelong pursuit, and trying to do it with a poor instructor is a frustrating waste of time and money.

A good instructor asks what you want to accomplish. They do not immediately try to change your entire shooting style to suit their own ideas, at least not without justifying it beyond a simple "I prefer it this way." Most important, a good instructor does not insist that they have found "The Way" and that every other shooting instructor in the world is wrong.

Everyone wants a simple answer, the key to good shooting, the one little thing they are doing wrong that, if corrected, will turn them into Lord Ripon on pheasants or a gold medal trap shooter. Some instructors offer such a magic solution. One instructor who advertises widely insists that, for a right-handed shooter, the proper stance is right foot forward. Every other instructor in the history of the world insists on leading with the left foot, in the natural fighting stance described above. So who's correct?

Then there are the instructors who want you to stand square on to the target, rather than at 45 degrees, and insist you need to chop an inch off your length of pull to accommodate this odd stance. Fine to try, if you have an adjustable stock, but not so great if it means shortening a piece of expensive walnut on an $80,000 Holland & Holland. Now *that* could be an expensive lesson!

Prospective students should look askance at such claims on the part of any instructor. Self-appointed messiahs may get decent results occasionally, but anyone who says they will have a beginner consis-

tently breaking 25 straight after one morning's instruction is selling snake oil.

Finally, be aware of the instructors who specialize in skeet, trap, or sporting clays and who will usually insist on a rigid stance with the student beginning their shooting with the gun at the shoulder, the eye aligned down the rib, and the safety off. This is all fine if you intend to shoot American trap or skeet and nothing else. The problem is that anyone who learns to shoot this way will have great difficulty later adapting to any other method. Just as a driver who learns to drive with an automatic transmission never seems able to adapt to a stick shift and a clutch, so learning to shoot "gun up, safety off" becomes so ingrained, you can never comfortably shoot "gun down, safety on." For a game shooter or anyone who wants to shoot game at some later date, this can be fatal. You do *not* walk in on a point with the gun at your shoulder and the safety off, nor do you stand in a shooting butt like that, waiting for driven grouse. For this reason, one of the most important motions in shooting is the smooth, efficient gun mount, while watching the target in the air. Learning to shoot gun-down teaches this mount and becomes the cornerstone of all your shooting.

* * *

The first recorded formal shooting school was set up near London, England, in the 1860s. By the 1880s, all the major London gun makers had shooting grounds of their own, where they tested and finished their guns and rifles and allowed clients to practice. When gun fitting became common, clients would go to the grounds to be fitted, using a try-gun (a fully functional shotgun with a stock that can be adjusted in every direction).

Gradually, courses of fire were set up, employing various types of thrown

Ryan Mason demonstrating proper stance and gun mounting. Ryan is an international skeet shooter, and the rules demand the gun be down until the bird is called for. Proper mounting is essential. Ryan likes to have his feet a little closer to 90 degrees to the target, rather than the usual 45 degrees. Weight is on the leading foot, and the gun comes up to the face. Notice that there's not a lot of change in his body from unmounted gun to mounted.

artificial targets, as well as the use of live birds. The final step was the formal course of instruction, with qualified instructors teaching newcomers how to use a shotgun, or working with experienced shooters to perfect their technique or solve problems. Just as even the best professional golfers realize they can always improve and take regular lessons, so the best shots continue to work with qualified instructors to improve their style.

The most famous American exhibition shooter of all time was Annie Oakley, the petite trick shot who performed with Buffalo Bill's Wild West Show. Oakley dazzled audiences across Europe with her rifle shooting skills; when the show reached London, all of England was soon at her feet. While Oakley was deadly with a rifle, however, she was not so good with a shotgun. During her stay in London, she paid a visit to Charles Lancaster & Co., on New Bond Street, where she met its proprietor, H.A.A. Thorn. Thorn was one of the leading figures in the London gun trade, a gun maker, inventor, shooting instructor, and author who liked to be called "Mr. Lancaster." As a result, Thorn's name does not have the renown it deserves.

Thorn undertook to fit Miss Oakley for a pair of shotguns, then gave her a series of lessons at his shooting ground. A natural shot, she was soon as devastating with a shotgun as with a rifle. She defeated her future husband in a box-pigeon match, and even gave lessons herself to English women who wanted to shoot, not just watch. For England in that era, this was a remarkable thing to do and the beginning of active participation by women in English shooting that endures to this day.

H.A.A. Thorn wrote a book called *The Art of Shooting*, which appeared in 1889, has gone through more than a dozen edi-

tions, and has been in print ever since. It is one of shooting's all-time best sellers, and deservedly so. Charles Lancaster & Co. built several guns for Annie Oakley and was her London gun maker from that point on. Oakley herself became an American heroine, and inspired movies, books, and a Broadway musical. Throughout her life, she was a strong advocate of women learning to shoot, for both sport and self-defense, and gave shooting instruction to an estimated 15,000 women during her lifetime.

The example of Annie Oakley illustrates a couple important points. One, most instructors agree that women are better shooting students than men. They accept both instruction and criticism better, because they have nothing to prove. The second is that women can also be better instructors than men, and for both male and female students. Shooting truly is a unisex sport; on any given day, a good female shooter can whip a good male shooter, and vice versa. The playing field is exactly

level in that respect—and you could also argue that women have an advantage in that they are not burdened with the male ego, when it comes to shooting prowess.

* * *

In days gone by, the accepted way for a young person to learn to shoot was to be introduced to guns at an early age, receive some instruction from a relative, be watched like a hawk and, if he made the grade, be gradually accepted into the company of hunters and shooters that made up his family. Robert Ruark's *The Old Man and the Boy* portrays this culture in an admittedly idealized way. Alas, that way of life is gone forever. Many people now grow up with no one in their family to impart the knowledge and skills of shooting. Others live in cities and have no local farmland where they can learn to shoot and practice in an informal way. Still others come to shooting later in life and attempt to acquire

skills that, while easy for a young person, are much more difficult for an adult.

Today, on a shooting range, you will encounter self-taught adults who are completely unaware of the fundamentals of shooting etiquette, and some who are certifiably dangerous with a gun. What's worse is finding yourself with such a person in a group, hunting pheasants or doves or shooting a round of skeet, activities where safety is a paramount concern, and there is no easy escape.

While we talk about learning to shoot well as a separate activity, we should really emphasize that what is important is learning to shoot safely. Indeed, the aspects of skill and safety should never be considered in isolation. Safe shotgun handling should go hand in hand with skillful shotgun handling, and the former should never, ever, under any circumstances, be sacrificed to the latter.

Professional shotgun instructors incorporate safe gun handling and proper etiquette into every aspect of their curriculum. This is not necessarily true of fathers, uncles, brothers, and boyfriends, even if they are safe gun handlers themselves. Some simply take it for granted or think the issue is self-evident. Self-taught shooters, who learned their technique from a book, often skip the chapter on safety and etiquette (if there is one).

There are a few simple rules of shotgun courtesy:

- Never touch another person's gun without first asking permission.
- On a range, do not offer advice unless it is asked for.
- Never comment on someone's performance while they are shooting, or attempt to tell them where they are missing.
- Never attempt to grab someone's gun out of his hands if they are having a problem, such as clearing a jam.
- When on the line in trap or in a squad

as found in skeet or sporting clays, do not laugh or talk loudly while someone else is shooting.

- Do not attempt to turn every shooting session into a competition, whether the other shooters want to or not.

One point to make regarding "where you are missing." It is possible to see a charge of shot in the air, and many experienced instructors can do so. It is best described as a "disturbance," a brief shimmer in the air, and can be seen better in some light conditions than others. Surprisingly, it is most often seen under "cloudy bright" conditions than it is in open sunlight.

At various times, shotshell manufacturers have offered "tracer" rounds that, theoretically, allow the shooter to see where their shot went. This has never worked very well, because, if you are looking to see where your shot goes, you are sure to miss. Instructors never found it particularly helpful either, and the fact that it set fire to dry grass was a definite drawback in hot climates. Being able to see conventional shot in the air, however, is almost a status symbol for would-be instructors, and many people claim to see it when, in fact, they don't. As for people who start loudly telling you your shot was behind or high or low, they are usually basing the assessment on the flight of the wad. Since a wad opens like a flower and flies like a demented frisbee, where it flew bears no relation to where your shot charge went. Such information, well meaning or not, is not helpful to the shooter, and onlookers would do better to just keep quiet, unless they are asked.

These are accepted courtesies, not hard rules, but, as you can see, most are merely adaptations of the Golden Rule: Do unto others, as you would have them do unto you.

* * *

There are instructors who also need a few lessons in good manners. Some come from military backgrounds and think every flat surface is a parade ground. Others believe the best way to spur effort is to humiliate someone, in a loud voice. Still others, finding themselves in a position of authority for the first time in their lives, immediately forget that they do not know everything there is to know.

In my observation, these afflictions never seem to apply to female instructors, most of whom believe you catch more flies with honey than vinegar and, so, take a very soft-spoken approach. One of the best all-around shooting instructors I have ever met is a diminutive lady named Il Ling New, who works as both a freelance and a staff instructor at Gunsite, in Arizona. Miss New specializes in tactical work, but also teaches hunting skills with rifles large and small, and tactical shotgun skills. Working with her on many occasions, I have never once heard her raise her voice. Then again, being as good with a gun as she is, she doesn't need to.

Loud and abusive behavior rarely gets good long-term results, but even a short-term acquaintance with such an instructor can be damaging. Before signing on for a series of lessons, it is beneficial to watch an instructor at work with someone else, or at least talk with a former student about his or her methods. Your choice of a shooting instructor could be the single most important decision you make on the road to becoming good with a shotgun.

This leads to one last point. Some instructors have an affinity for a particular type of shotgun. If they happen to prefer over/unders and you show up with a side-by-side, you do not want them to immediately start denigrating your choice of gun or blaming it for every miss. Assuming the dimensions are acceptable, it is possible to shoot very well with any decent gun, whether it is a brand-new semi-auto,

Alison Caselman demonstrating stance and gun mounting. Alison keeps her feet closer to 45 degrees and holds her right elbow higher than Ryan does. Her stance and technique are excellent, with her weight well forward, her body relaxed, and, so, she is able to respond to any target. Alison has the most piercing "predator's gaze" when she mounts her gun, a sure sign of concentration, an essential element in shotgun shooting.

your father's 50-year-old pump gun, or a century-old side-by-side.

One time, I spent a couple days with a prominent instructor who was a good guy overall, a very fine shot, and a dedicated student of the shotgun. He and his wife both shot heavy sporting over/unders. I was carrying a Grulla Armas side-by-side that I'd had made in Spain; it is a 12-bore built on a 20-gauge frame and weighs six pounds, five ounces. In it, I shoot very light loads. For two days, every time I missed a clay, I heard that it was the fault of that "girlie gun" I was shooting, followed by a suggestion that he could get me a deal on a "real" gun like a Browning.

A good instructor will work with the gun you bring, unless it is so completely unsuitable by weight, dimensions, or choke that the student is at a real disadvantage. Some shooting grounds have shotguns

available for loan. But know that, while you might appear with a perfectly nice over/under 28-gauge, there are some instructors who will immediately insist you switch to a 12- or 20-gauge semi-auto. To me, any semi-auto is a poor gun with which to learn, because it is mechanically more complicated, inherently less safe (especially in the hands of someone not very familiar with guns), and more prone to difficulties such as jams or failures to eject. Generally, the safety is not in the most convenient spot for shooting safety-on. The reduced recoil of a semi-auto, which is really its only virtue for a beginner, does not begin to compensate for the drawbacks.

GUN FITTING

Because a shotgun does not have conventional sights like a rifle, whether it

delivers its pattern where you want it to depends largely on how well the gun fits you.

As mentioned before, gun fit is more important than some would have us believe, but not as important as others insist. A good shot can do quite well with a poorly fitting gun, and a bad shot will miss even if the gun fits perfectly. In the former case, however, the good shot knows where the gun falls short and compensates for it. This requires awareness and conscious effort. At the end of a long day of shooting, whether at trap, driven birds, or flighting doves, when every muscle is tired and the mind is weary, having a properly fitted gun that allows good shooting without extraneous effort pays dividends. Proper fit is at its most valuable in game shooting, particularly in reacting to the totally unexpected.

The concept of gun fit originated in the 1860s, as shotguns became more refined. At first, a buyer would try several different guns off the shelf, pick the one that seemed most comfortable, measure the di-mensions, and proceed accordingly. Then came the idea of shooting several different guns at targets. Eventually, William Jones of Birmingham patented the first adjustable "try gun," a working firearm with a stock that was adjustable for length, drop, and cast. With a try gun, the client accompanies the gun fitter to a shooting range and proceeds to fire a hundred shots or more, with the fitter adjusting each aspect of the stock until he arrives at the perfect fit for the client's needs.

Like shooting, gun fitting is a skill. Anyone can claim to be a gun fitter—and many do—but really competent gun fitters are few and far between. To be properly measured, you need a fitter with several different try guns; you also need several hours on a range, a few hundred rounds of ammunition, a proper patterning plate, a variety of moving and stationary targets, and three or four hundred dollars in your pocket. There is no way you can obtain anything but a rudimentary idea of your

measurements with a tape measure in a gun shop, or by filling out a chart of body measurements, or by standing at some gun maker's booth at a show and stretching out your arms.

There are several aspects to gun fit above and beyond your body size. First is whether you are right- or left-handed, as well as whether your right or left eye is your "master" eye. Many books and articles have attempted to show an easy way of determining eye domination. A simple way is to put your hands together to form a triangular opening at arm's length, center an object in the opening with both eyes open, then slowly pull your hands toward you. You hands will naturally come back to your master eye.

This is helpful, but not absolute. Your master eye can shift permanently as you age, and eye dominance can even change back and forth in the course of a day, because of fatigue. Sometimes, it will shift temporarily because of an irritation.

Anyone with shifting eye dominance can solve the problem by simply shutting one eye. This eliminates depth perception, however, and narrows your field of vision, neither of which help your shooting—but, then, neither of these effects is as outright damaging to accurate shooting as a complete change of eye dominance. A good gun fitter will pay close attention to eye dominance, and a competent instructor can even identify eye dominance issues from watching a series of shots.

* * *

Standard shotgun dimensions today are roughly as follows: The length of pull is 14 inches, drop at comb 1½ inches, drop at heel 2½ inches, with no cast (bend to left or right) either way. Almost anyone can adapt to these dimensions and shoot pretty well. Some very good shots go through their entire lives shooting factory guns with standard dimensions and, especially

if they stick to just one gun, can reach a point where it would be hard to improve very much.

Not everyone is average, however, and, for the very short, very tall, those with extra long arms, and those with some sort of physical abnormality, stock alterations can be made—most of them fairly easily and cheaply. It is not necessary to spend $5,000 to have a gun restocked in order to get dimensions close to what you need. The key, however, is first determining what exactly you do need. Money spent on a proper gun fitting is never wasted, especially if you intend to buy a custom-built shotgun. Too, if you can find a shooting club with a good instructor who knows shotguns and has a selection of different guns to try—different gauges, actions, and dimensions—then you can experiment a little before making a decision about which gun to buy or whether to change from what you already have.

Although it was mentioned before, it bears saying again: *No one can get measured in any meaningful way unless they already know how to shoot reasonably well.* Sometimes an instructor will take a new student, even a complete beginner, and start padding the stock with foam rubber and tape to build it into "proper" dimensions, this before the student fires more than a dozen shots. Sometimes this is justified—if the gun in question is far off normal dimensions, for example—but often, it is just an exercise in the instructor showing how much he knows. Personally, I would think twice before allowing a total stranger to start taping up the nice walnut stock on my father's old gun, and for sure he's not going to go at it with a saw or a rasp.

CHAPTER 12

NOTES AND OBSERVATIONS

A Grulla Armas 12-gauge, is light at six pounds, five ounces. It was built on a 20-gauge frame, with 29-inch barrels, and performs best with lighter loads, such as these Gamebore English shells.

The last chapter of a book such as this one is a funny thing. The author's predecessors on this path, many of them dead for a century or more now, would often find themselves at the end, having covered their subject in a logical manner, chapter by chapter, yet realizing there was much of importance still unwritten. This usually included the author's final thoughts on the subject and their conclusions drawn from observation and experience that just didn't seem to fit anywhere else. It was also the final opportunity for the author to let his hair down, so to speak, and tell it straight, without apology, without worrying about

offending anyone. For some reason, the subjects in question seemed to be the sensitive ones—women and shooting, Damascus barrels, or the deceptive trap of velocity. The final chapter was where the author could finally and irrevocably get it off their chest, then or never. So, as it was with those before me, it is now my turn.

DAMASCUS BARRELS

There is no topic more certain of igniting a controversy, if not a fistfight, than the subject of Damascus barrels and whether they are safe to shoot. Since about

Blackpowder proof marks on an E.M. Reilly from 1890s.

Fine English Damascus barrels, found on a Gibbs & Pitt's gun from the 1870s.

A Damascus barrel blackpowder proof mark on an E.M. Reilly shotgun.

1930, Damascus has been systematically demonized by the shooting industry, as well as by several generations of gun writers. It has been condemned as a death trap, a material rendered unsafe by a combination of years of insidious internal deterioration and the high pressures of modern cartridges. To read the words of some writers, most notably my old friend Michael McIntosh, you would think that even being in the same room with a set of Damascus barrels and a box of smokeless shotshells was putting your life at risk. McIntosh wasn't alone. Browse some back issues of *Gun Digest* or any of the outdoor magazines and you will find warnings that no gun with Damascus barrels should ever be fired, with any ammunition, under any condition. To do so will mean almost certain maiming, blinding, or death.

Before we go any further, perhaps we should explain exactly what Damascus steel is.

In the early years of centerfire shotguns, most barrels, and all really fine ones, were made from material commonly called Damascus steel, also known as twist or, sometimes, laminated steel. There were different types and they had different names, but the principle was the same: Instead of being made from a solid bar of steel with a hole bored through it, the barrel was made by wrapping strips of metal around a mandrel and then welding the seams.

The strips themselves were made by welding alternate strips of iron and steel to form a rod, twisting it into a tight spiral, hammering it flat, and then repeating the process of twisting and hammering. This resulted in the distinctive—and quite lovely—wavy pattern that is the hallmark

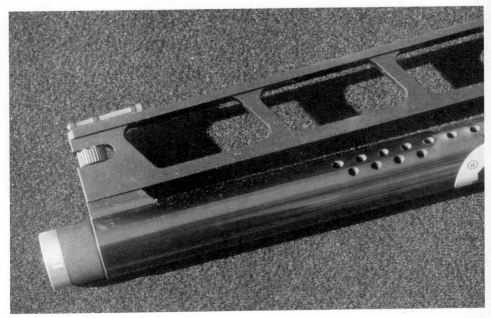

A trap rib and muzzle brake on a Browning Cynergy).

of Damascus. All the finest gun makers used Damascus steel in preference to the fluid steel bars then available, because early fluid steel contained air pockets, weak spots, and impurities.

Making Damascus barrels is a highly skilled art, and the very best ones came from Belgium and France. English Damascus could be very good, but gun makers like Boss and Woodward preferred the best Belgian, because of the consistent high quality. Damascus barrels came in different grades, usually priced according to the number of rods (or stubs) used in creating the strips. Hence, we have two-stub, three-stub, and even up to six or seven stubs. It was generally acknowledged, however, that anything more than three tended to reverse the process, and, while exceedingly fancy, the six- or seven-stub Damascus was not as strong as three-stub.

Sir Joseph Whitworth, the English industrialist and steel maker, made the breakthrough that moved fluid steel ahead of Damascus once and for all, when he

An E.M. Reilly gun with Damascus barrels and B&P High Pheasant cartridges. A match made in heaven.

The author hunting with E.M. Reilly with Damascus barrels.

developed the process of condensing molten steel to force out the air pockets. The result was a steel bar that was uniform, strong, and ultimately cheaper than Damascus. Boss and Purdey were early adherents of Whitworth fluid condensed steel, although all the best gun makers continued to use both.

Tests carried out under rigorous conditions to see which were superior were inconclusive. The fact is, good Damascus is superior to good fluid steel in some ways, while fluid steel is superior in others. There is no point getting into a debate over which is better. My point is only that Damascus was perfectly safe in the past, can still be safe, and has many virtues. A fine gun fitted with Damascus barrels can have an exquisite balance that most fluid steel barrels only dream of.

Modern tests carried out by some independent writers, in which old guns with Damascus barrels were subjected to ungodly charges of smokeless powder and still refused to give up the ghost, have not laid to rest the idea that Damascus is inherently dangerous. One theory is that, around 1930, needing to sell guns, America's ammunition makers (who happened to be connected to gun companies), got the idea that people would buy new guns if they could convince them that their old guns were unsafe with modern ammunition. The timing for this theory is certainly right, and gun and ammunition companies have never balked at whatever tactics deemed necessary to sell their wares.

At one point, in recent years, the proprietor of a large retail shooting operation suggested such a test to a magazine editor. He would provide 25 or 30 old guns with Damascus barrels, they would be tested under laboratory conditions, and the results would be reported in the magazine, which was one of the country's largest. The editorial director agreed, but only—*only*—if the test showed Damascus to be dangerous. If the Damascus guns passed the test, he didn't want the story. That tells you something about the relationship between gun magazines and the industry they serve.

B&P Competition One loads are beautifully suited to lighter 12-gauge guns, such as this custom Grulla Armas at six pounds, five ounces.

Vintage gun-cleaning implements.

Because this anti-Damascus campaign began in the 1930s, many of today's shooters grew up being warned about Damascus by their father or grandfather, and words of wisdom from such a source can be unassailable. You don't cast aspersions on a man's mother's virtue or question his father's knowledge of guns, no matter how fatuous those views might be.

The essence of the argument against Damascus is that, being made from strips of metal with welds, there could be tiny weak spots, or moisture trapped inside, eating through the steel invisibly, from the inside out. Exactly how moisture could be "trapped" in a pocket of red-hot steel I'm not sure, but that's the theory. There are ways of telling if a set of barrels is sound, and a good gunsmith knows how to do it. Far be it from me to recommend that anyone go out and shoot an old gun with modern ammunition,

no matter what the barrels are made of, but if a good barrel man says they're sound, then, as my gun maker friend Edy von Atzigen once said to me, "A good set of barrels is a good set of barrels. It doesn't matter if they are Damascus or fluid steel."

There is another favorite canard of some under-educated gun writers, and that is the idea of "faux Damascus," or false Damascus. This idea is that, in the dim distant past, some gun makers painted fluid steel barrels to *look* like Damascus, because it was considered the mark of a fine gun. If you find one of these, they say, they are perfectly safe to shoot.

There are so many flaws in that line of thinking it's hard to know where to start. Consider this: You're a gun maker turning out low-priced guns for the henhouse market. You need to keep costs down by any means possible. Yet you hire a skilled artist

B&P light competition loads. They perform well in older shotguns.

to paint fake Damascus markings on barrels to make them more attractive? Have you ever looked at a good Damascus pattern, and asked yourself how it might be artificially reproduced on fluid steel, in a way that would last more than one session at the range? It would not be simple. Even if you were trying to make a cheap gun look good and sell it for more money, it would not be worth the trouble and additional expense.

Now, how would you tell if a barrel was "faux" Damascus? According to one (former) national gun columnist, you look down the bore. If you can't see the Damascus pattern, then the barrels are, in reality, fluid steel. Wrong, wrong, and wrong again. The Damascus pattern shows only on the exterior, because it is specially treated with acid to bring it out for the sake of aesthetics. A genuine Damascus bore is as uniform and shiny as any Whitworth steel barrel, or any modern chrome-moly or nickel-steel barrel, for that matter.

At one point, I asked three prominent dealers in really fine rifles and shotguns if they had ever, in all their years, seen a gun come along that had true "faux Damascus" barrels. The answer was no.

This is not to say that barrels do not exist that are made to look like Damascus, because there are some historical instances of this. In Belgium, right after the Great War, some barrels were faked, because there was no genuine Damascus available. And, by the way, we should mention that the trade in fine Damascus died largely because of the Great War. Germany occupied Belgium, including the gun making area around Liège, and left it in tatters. However, the genuine instances of such deceptions are tiny compared to the number of claims of "faux" Damascus by unscrupulous sellers and gullible writers.

* * *

The fuzzy stuff is tow, a wool from the hemp plant, and it is the mainstay of old English shotgun cleaning procedure. Wrapped around a jag, it scrubs bores by getting under fouling. It dates from the days of blackpowder, but works wonderfully well today—if you can find it!

Many very fine guns have been butchered in the name of safety, as a result of the anti-Damascus campaign. Some have been lined with steel tubes, which usually reduces the bore size by one; a 12 becomes a 16, a 16 becomes a 20, etc. Others have been sleeved, a process wherein the barrel tubes are cut off just forward of the forcing cone and replaced by fluid-steel tubes. Done by a skilled man, sleeving is almost invisible.

In my opinion, such action should only be taken as a last resort, and I say that as someone who owns four shotguns and a rifle with Damascus barrels. All are extremely high quality and shoot beautifully. The shotguns are three 12s and a 16, and all except one have 30-inch barrels. (I have another 12 that was sleeved—sob!—and I console myself with the knowledge that, had it been original, I could never have afforded it; it's a J. Woodward & Sons.) Pick up any one of those shotguns and heft it in

A vintage English oil bottle, filled with vintage English oil. Nothing elaborate, but it still works very well.

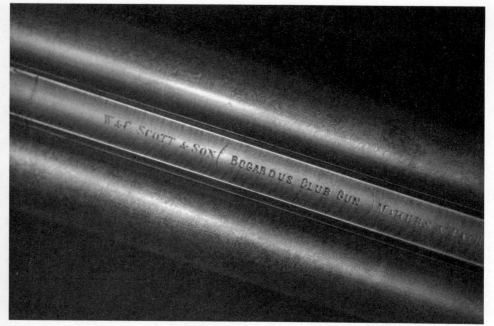

Damascus barrels on a W&C Scott gun made for export to the U.S., for Capt. Adam Bogardus, a famous shooter connected with some duck hunting camps on the Mississippi.

Federal Paper shotshells, made now for competition, work equally well on game birds such as doves, grouse, pheasants, and quail. The gun is a Charles Lancaster.

the hands, mount it to the shoulder, drop it, mount it again. Then pick up another gun and compare the balance and liveliness. The difference is noticeable.

I have also read that fluid steel was an improvement on Damascus, because the barrel walls could be thinner and, therefore, lighter. That has not been my experience—quite the opposite, in fact. Damascus barrels all seem lighter and livelier than comparable fluid steel. They also have certain qualities of resilience and ductility that fluid steel does not have. Fluid steel, if it ruptures, does so lengthwise; Damascus cannot do that because it has no longitudinal grain. Instead, the straps tend to stretch, which translates into a bulge, not a split.

In one instance, the great gun maker Stephen Grant took a Damascus barrel that had been bulged by the shooter accidentally dropping in a 20-gauge cartridge, then load-

Elaborate adjustable high rib and muzzle brake on a Galazan (CSMC) A-10 trap gun.
Photo by John Giammatteo

Adjustable rib, muzzle brake, and interchangeable choke tubes with integral brakes, on CSMC A-10 competition gun.
Photo by John Giammatteo

ing a 12-gauge shotshell behind it. Note I said the barrel bulged. It did not burst. Grant simply hammered it back down to its proper dimensions and returned it to its owner.

A comprehensive test of Damascus versus fluid steel barrels was carried out, in 1891, by the Birmingham Proof House, subjecting 39 sets of barrels of different material to progressively heavier proof loads. Damascus lasted the longest and took three of the top four places. Whitworth fluid condensed steel placed second.

As you can see, the question of which material is superior has continued for well over a century. Fluid steel in its various forms and alloys certainly triumphed, but it was less a triumph of overall quality than of availability and cost. At first, Whitworth steel was more expensive than even the best Damascus, and gun makers like Boss charged a premium of up to £3 for Whitworth barrels on a gun that cost £50. That's a hefty percentage. In fact, it's about the same amount they paid their engravers, the Sumner family, for completely engraving a Boss game gun!

As fluid steel alloys became better and better and rival processes sprang up to challenge Whitworth, prices came down. Meanwhile, the making of Damascus (which is an ancient and highly skilled art), declined and prices went up.

Some years ago, a director of James Purdey told me that, if they could obtain proper Damascus barrels today, they could sell every gun they could make. Alas, the making of Damascus for gun barrels is a lost art.

PROOF

The European countries all have proof houses and proof laws for firearms that do not exist in the United States. They date back to the proving of armor and all have a long history. The history of proof in Europe was covered in great detail in a series in *Gun Digest*, in the 1950s, by A. Baron Engelhardt, and in a later series by Lee Kennett. The common reference on proof is *The Standard Dictionary of Proof Marks*, by Gerhard Wirnsberger. For details on English proof, Nigel Brown's three-volume *British Gunmakers* includes both historical and modern proof markings and practice.

In a nutshell, a proof house is a quasi-governmental body charged with the responsibility of testing guns for strength before they are sold. Gun makers submit guns under construction, which are tested with over-strength shells; this is a provisional proof and is followed by definitive proof when the gun is finished. Proof marks are stamped on both the barrels and action, showing such information as chamber length, maximum tested pressure, choke or the lack thereof, and bore diameter. Over the years, proof marks have become more numerous and the information they convey far more detailed.

Proof laws in Europe are very strict, and no gun dealer can sell a gun that is "out of proof." A gun goes out of proof for any number of reasons, including having its chamber lengthened or the bore diameter

exceed the marked diameter, the latter indicating excessive wear to the barrel walls. Such a gun must be sent back for reproofing before it can be sold at retail. A gun that was originally proofed only with blackpowder can be sent for nitro proof, which would then allow it to be sold as a gun suitable for shooting modern ammunition.

The U.S. has no such proof laws. Proving guns (as opposed to the legal "proofing") was left to the individual companies on the laudable, but somewhat dubious assumption that it was not in their interest to sell dangerous products and, so, they would not deliberately do so. In the case of old American guns, such as Parkers with Damascus barrels, the buyer has no way of telling from the markings what modern loads it might or might not accept safely.

Anyone thinking of buying an old European gun is well advised to learn something about proof and proof marks before spending any money. Many English guns have been brought into the United States with 2½-inch chambers, which were then lengthened to 2¾ inches, to accept standard American ammunition. This applies to 20- and 28-gauge guns, as well as 12s. In most cases, this procedure is safe enough, although it does nothing for the resale value and may damage the shooting qualities. However, in Europe, such an alteration requires a trip to the proof house, to be reproofed with longer shotshells. In America, very few of these guns are reproofed, because that would mean shipping them back to Europe at great trouble and expense. Since it is not legally required here, why bother?

Measuring the chamber with a pocket chamber gauge and then comparing that information with the gun's pedigree stamped on the barrel flats can tell you a great deal about where a gun's been and what it's done. Learning to measure bore diameter and barrel wall thickness is also useful. Bore diameter, taken nine inches from the

The action flats of a custom-made Pedro Arrizabalaga gun, from the year 2000. Modern guns have many proof marks, showing everything from the date of manufacture to the gauge, barrel diameters, and chamber length.

breech, is stamped on the barrel flats. Any discrepancy can tell you what kind of loads have been put through the gun and gives you a pretty good idea of life expectancy.

While some dealers are honest and knowledgeable, many have sprung up in recent years who know little or nothing about the old guns they are selling, and know as much about proofing and proof marks as they do about the chemical composition of rocket fuel. If they don't know what these proof marks mean, then you need to.

MODERN AMMUNITION VARIETIES

Compared to the state of affairs in 1970, the modern shotgunner has an embarrassment of riches, when it comes to ammunition. Not only are the Big Three—Federal, Remington and Winchester—producing a wider variety of loads than before and in most gauges, ammunition is regularly imported from other countries, and several small specialty ammunition makers have sprung up in the United States to serve niche markets.

Most of the importers or specialty makers offer something that can be found nowhere else, and that is the basis of the attraction. For example, Baschieri & Pellagri, the Italian ammunition company that has been around since 1885, loads shotshells using the Gordon system's compressible base wad. This noticeably reduces felt recoil. That is not the company's only claim to fame, but it's a good start. B&P also offers a superb all-around 12-gauge game load (High Pheasant), a fine pigeon load (Star Rossa), and a variety of others in every gauge, including some excellent 16-gauge loads.

Kent Cartridge of England, which also owns Gamebore, imports a variety of shotshells that range from excellent competition

A Perazzi MX28B 28-gauge game gun, with B&P 28-gauge "Extra Rossa" loads. This is a hard-hitting, fast-handling combination.

loads to blackpowder shotshells and non-lead tungsten-matrix for use on migratory birds.

In the U.S., RST has made a specialty of loading ammunition for older guns, guns with shorter chambers, and guns requiring lower pressures, such as blackpowder-proof guns or those with Damascus barrels. RST offers a variety of loads with paper hulls, including a line of pigeon loads, which, while in the classic "1¼ to 3¼" configuration, offer a choice of three different muzzle velocities and are easier on both the shoulder and the ears than a standard pigeon load. Shooters of English guns with 2½-inch chambers love RSTs, whether the shells are in 12-, 16-, 20-, or 28-gauge.

Another interesting company is Polywad, which began by manufacturing components for handloaders wanting "spreader" loads and ended up by making complete "Spred-R" ammunition. A spreader load is one that will give a quick, wide pattern, even in a Modified or Full choke gun. These were necessary in the days before interchangeable choke tubes became common, because a large number of American shotguns had Full choke barrels. A spreader is created by placing a small plastic plug in among the pellets, which causes the shot charge to break apart as soon as it leaves the muzzle. Polywad also makes such disparate products as 2-inch 12-gauge ammunition for light English 12s with short chambers, and innovative slug designs, such as its Quik-Shok slug that breaks into three parts on impact.

As shooters get more deeply into shooting and start looking for either better loads for their particular application or specialty loads for particular purposes, it is wise to look beyond the conventional companies and examine what is available from smaller firms. In many ways, smaller companies are driving the evolution of the shotshell today, just as they always have. Equally important, they are producing ammunition for which there is not a mass market demand—RST is the best example of this—and allowing owners of older guns to continue shooting and hunting with them.

RECOIL AND SHOT CHARGE

How severely a gun recoils depends on three factors: the weight of the shot charge, the shot charge's velocity when it leaves the muzzle, and the weight of the shotgun. While recoil can be moderated by altering any of the above, by far the easiest way is to reduce the weight of the shot charge. Increasing the weight of the gun is not an immediate option, and a certain minimum velocity is required to give a good pattern and firm impact on the target. If, however, you find that your 1⅛-ounce load at 1,100 fps is stinging you, the simplest and easiest thing to do is go to a one-ounce, or even a ⅞-ounce load and see if that solves the problem.

All the big makers of volume trap and skeet loads offer virtually the same load at one-ounce as they do at 1⅛, and many trap shooters who fear the onset of a flinch will go to the lighter load as an immediate remedy. Often, they find their scores do not suffer in the least and stick with the lighter load from that point on. For handloaders, an added benefit of using fewer pellets is significantly lower cost.

Because smaller-gauge guns are lighter than 12s, they potentially all have the same problem. In the 16, sticking with a one-ounce or ⅞-ounce load will help with a gun weighing in at six pounds. In a 20-gauge at 5½ pounds, either ⅞- or ¾-ounce loads are the ticket to keep recoil from being unpleasant. Even a 28-gauge, believe it or not, can kick sharply, when you put a heavy load into a really light gun. Every shotgun has a point at which its recoil becomes sharp and unfriendly. Stay on the right side of that line and you will have fun shooting. Cross it and shooting will quickly become an ordeal, along with increased flinching and missed targets.

MUZZLE BRAKES AND OTHER DEVICES

A muzzle brake is simply a device on the muzzle of a gun that redirects powder gases to offset the jet effect, thereby reducing recoil or muzzle jump. On a shotgun, most take the form of a pattern of holes drilled in the barrel near the muzzle. Depending on the angle at which they are drilled, they will expel gases either to pull the gun forward or push the muzzles down.

This sounds like the perfect solution for excessive recoil, but it isn't. For one thing, almost all muzzle brakes increase muzzle blast. This is fine, if you wear hearing protection, which everyone should in any non-hunting situation, but, if you are standing on a line with a trap squad, blast out to the side is annoying to the shooter next to you. Aside from the noise, the shockwave is also disconcerting to anyone standing near the muzzle. Ear protection may protect you from the noise, but nothing protects you from the shock.

Another approach to taming recoil is some sort of spring-loaded butt pad, or internal inertia recoil reducer loaded with mercury. All of these have an effect, but it is not always what you might like. The mercury recoil reducer in the stock gurgles, which is mildly annoying; worse, it is heavy and changes the balance of the gun. As for the spring-loaded, shock-absorbing pad, this has also been tried in different forms over many years. Some people feel they help and quite like them. Others find them disconcerting to have the gun recoil in their hands, but feel no push against their shoulder, and this takes some getting used to.

The basic problem is that, in ballistics, there is no free lunch. The law of the equal and opposite reaction has not been and cannot be repealed. So, every foot-pound of energy created by the shotshell must be coped with, compensated for, dissipated, or diverted in some way. In this manner, a muzzle brake converts this energy from a

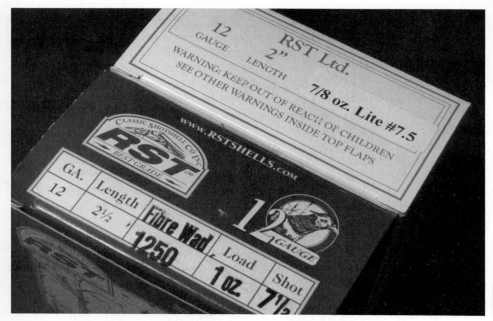

RST is an American company that makes a wide variety of excellent specialty ammunition, including rarities like 2-inch 12-gauge and 2½-inch 16-gauge.

shove against the shoulder and a rap on the cheek into an assault on the ears.

In fairness, I must say that muzzle brakes have progressed considerably over the past 20 years. Today, some brake patterns do reduce recoil significantly without turning the muzzle blast into an ear-rending clap of thunder, but any muzzle brake that purports to handle recoil with no increase at all in noise is not being marketed truthfully. There is, too, an in-between level of muzzle brake that works purely to tame muzzle jump; since muzzle jump is truly the problem that needs to be addressed, because it both results in a bruised cheek and enhances being able to get back on target quickly for a second shot, this is a worthwhile improvement. Gases are directed upwards, rather than to the rear, so any increase in noise can be kept to a minimum. By far, however, the easiest way to deal with the equal and opposite reaction is to reduce the initial action by going to a lighter load.

VELOCITY AND THE SHOT PELLET

Compared to a streamlined rifle bullet, the shotgun's round lead pellets do not retain velocity well at all, and the faster a pellet leaves the muzzle, the faster it slows down. So, an increase in muzzle velocity of 100 fps does not translate into a 100 fps increase in corresponding energy at 40 yards; instead of 100 fps more at 40 yards, it might be down to 50. In return for that increased velocity, the shooter has taken the increased whack on the shoulder when the gun was fired, yet has not gained a commensurate increase in killing power out where the bird is.

The larger and heavier a pellet is, the better it retains its velocity. Knowing this, English shooters in the 1920s experimented with using very large pellets for waterfowl and increasing the shot charge weight in order to gain more pellets, then offsetting the increase in recoil by deliberately reducing the velocity. They found that, even at velocities as low as 850 fps at the muzzle, they were still getting kills at 60 to 80 yards from their big waterfowling guns, because the heavy pellets did not slow down as much as a smaller pellet would.

Keep in mind, these were *big* waterfowl guns, including punt guns up to 2- or 1-gauge. Still, this is an important concept to keep in mind, when choosing ammunition for any purpose, whether game or clays: It may start out fast, with the resulting increase in recoil, noise, and diminished pattern quality, but what do you get in return when the pellets reach the target?

Some clays shooters insist that a faster load gets the pellets to the target more quickly, thereby reducing the lead (forward allowance) required to hit it, even if the pellets themselves don't have much of this increased velocity left when they arrive. The difference in required lead, however, is slight, a few inches at the most. If a shot charge averages 1,000 fps over a 33-yard (100-foot) distance, which is a reasonable range for either a live bird or a clay, then it covers that distance in .10-second. If it averages 1,200 fps, then it covers it in .08-second. The difference is .02-second. During those two one-hundredths of a second, a bird flying at 30 mph will cover about 10 inches. In the split-second determination of forward allowance with a shot pattern, 10 inches at 33 yards is completely inconsequential.

Increased velocity is a deceptive siren. It cannot and will not compensate for poor shooting. In fact, pursued indiscriminately, it may make your shooting worse.

CLEANING SHOTGUNS

With modern shotshells, smokeless powder, and non-corrosive primers, cleaning your shotgun is no longer the critical concern it was in days past. Many a gun goes for weeks, months, or even years without seeing a cleaning rod or a drop of Hoppe's No. 9. The exception is the semi-auto, whose mechanism-operating gas ports get clogged regardless the ammunition. As well, all metal parts need lubrication to function reliably and to avoid long-term damage.

Whether it is strictly necessary from a corrosion point of view, it is a good idea to clean any gun on a regular basis, if for no other reason than to run your eye and hands over the working parts and head off problems. Metal parts sustain wear and screws become loose. It's best to catch little problems before they become big ones.

Guns also pick up grit, especially in windy, dusty conditions, and this grit can mix with oil or gun grease to create a grinding compound that would do a machine shop proud. With break-action guns, it is important to keep the hinge mechanism clean and greased, and lubrication is also important for the ejectors.

Oil and grease are not interchangeable. Oil both lubricates and protects metal from rust, while grease is purely a lubricant. Grease holds its lubricating oil in a non-migrating suspension. Oil likes to move around (often into areas where it isn't wanted, such as the stock), but grease will stay put and do its job. Generally, not much of either is needed. A dab here, a drop there, and regular inspections will do the trick.

Some years ago, there was great consternation among shotgunners at the build-up of plastic fouling in bores, resulting from the use of plastic shot cups. Shooters spent hours scrubbing, trying to get it out. The fear was that moisture could be trapped under this fouling and cause rust. This is a phenomenon I have only heard about and never seen, and I suspect more damage was actually done by over-zealous scrubbing with metal brushes.

There is a class of shotgunner who turns the cleaning of his precious totem into a religious act, replete with ritual, mysterious unguents and even gentle chanting. If this amuses anyone, then I'm all for it. It should be noted, however, that excessive cleaning can be as damaging as too little. Taking guns to pieces over and over results in wear, gradual loosening of the tight fit of certain parts, and buggered screws ("buggered" is the technical term for wrecking the notches on screw heads). Unless you know what you're doing, especially with intricate mechanisms like modern trigger groups, stick to the obvious cleaning and take your fine gun, once a year, to a professional gunsmith for a proper strip and clean.

FURTHER STUDY

As I wrap up this chapter, I am assailed by all the little bits and pieces of arcane and fascinating shotgun lore that somehow did not find their way into this book. For those who want to delve further, there are many specialized books that cover every aspect of shotguns in great detail. Many are old and out of print, but well worth searching out.

Major Sir Gerald Burrard's three-volume *The Modern Shotgun* is the unrivalled bible on double guns. Anything by Gough Thomas (G.T. Garwood) is worth finding, and Charles Lancaster's (H.A.A. Thorn) *The Art of Shooting* has been in print for 130 years and deservedly so. Sir Ralph Payne-Gallwey's *High Pheasants in Theory and Practice* is a century old this year, but still invaluable for the wingshooter in its examination of what kills and what does not. W.W. Greener's *The Gun and its Development* contains masses of interesting information, once you accept the fact that Greener had many professional axes

to grind. If you want to go off the deep end, there is a three-volume set on English gun patents by Crudgington and Baker— but let's rein ourselves in here.

Donald Dallas is a modern historian who has written official histories of several of the best English gun makers. His *The British Sporting Gun and Rifle* (2008) is a treasure, and anyone interested in the history of shotgun development should own it. For the English gun specialist, Nigel Brown's massive three-volume set, *British Gunmakers*, will keep you fascinated through entire vacations.

Among modern American shotgun writers, Michael McIntosh's books, especially *Best Guns*, tells the stories of good shotguns from all over the world, and Bob Brister's *Shotgunning: The Art and the Science* looks at the technical and practical aspects of the shooting itself, rather than the guns. Although not a shotgun specialist, Jack O'Connor's *The Shotgun Book* is valuable as a snapshot of how attitudes and guns were changing through the 1960s.

There are any number of books either written by gun makers (such as Edgar Harrison, Lancaster, or Robert Churchill), or about individual companies. There are other books devoted to a particular national industry, such as my own *Spanish Best*, which is a history of the fine gun trade in the Basque region of Spain. My other shotgun book, *Vintage British Shotguns*, looks at the less well-known names in the English trade and is a guide for Americans wanting an English gun.

For the romance of shotguns and the sheer joy of wingshooting, J.K. Stanford stands alone in my estimation. His volume *The Complex Gun* may become your constant companion, as it is mine.